Front Office Handbook

OrangeBooks Publication

1st Floor, Rajhans Arcade, Mall Road, Kohka, Bhilai, Chhattisgarh - 490020

Website: **www.orangebooks.in**

© **Copyright, 2024, Author**

All rights reserved. No part of this book may be reproduced, stored in a retrieval system, or transmitted, in any form by any means, electronic, mechanical, magnetic, optical, chemical, manual, photocopying, recording or otherwise, without the prior written consent of its writer.

First Edition, 2024

ISBN: 978-93-6554-199-1

FRONT OFFICE HANDBOOK

DR. VIVEK PATHAK

OrangeBooks Publication
www.orangebooks.in

Content

1. Introduction To Hospitality Industry 1
2. Classification of Hotels 3
3. Star Classification 7
4. Front Desk Layout and Equipment 12
5. Front Officer Organization 15
6. The Guest Cycle 20
7. Types of Rooms 22
8. Rate Categories 23
9. Front Office Systems 25
10. Property Management System 28
11. Reservation 31
12. Registration 47
13. Visa Rules And Regulations 57
14. Bell Desk Activities 64
15. Front Office Communication 71
16. Front Office Security 75
17. Guest Services 82
18. Checkout And Settlement Process 86
19. Night Audit 93
20. Front Office Accounting System 100
21. Handling Situations 105
22. Managing Hospitality 107
23. Planning And Evaluating Operations 116
24. Yield Management 125
25. In-House Sales 132
26. Front Desk Statistics 136
27. Glossary 138
28. Appendices 158

Introduction To Hospitality Industry

Definition of The Term "Hotel"

Hotel is defined by British law as a place where a bonafide traveller receives food and shelter, provided he is in a position to pay for it and is in a fit condition to be received. (Rights of admission reserved).

Hospitality is a part of larger enterprise known as travel and tourism industry. The travel and tourism is a vast group of business with one goal in common providing necessary and desired products and services to customers and travellers.

Accommodation facilities constitute a vital and fundamental part of tourism supply. Among the important inputs, which flow into the tourism system, is tourism accommodation forming a vital component of tourism superstructure.

A Hotel may be defined as an establishment whose primary business is providing lodging facilities for the general public and which furnishes one or more of the following.

Growth And Development of Hotel Industry

The hotel industry is perhaps one of the oldest industries in the world with establishment of money sometime in the 6th century B.C came the first real impetus (enterprise) for people of trade and travel prior to that it was difficult due to a lack of a standardized medium of exchange. The earliest Inns were ventures by husband and wife who used to provide modest wholesome food, quench thirst (mainly wine) and a large hall to stay for travellers against money. Initially, inns were called "Public Houses or Pubs" and the guests were called "Paying Guests".

These conditions remained for several hundred years. The advent of industrial revolution brought ideas and processes and progress in the business of Inn keeping. The development of railways and ships made traveling more prominent The industrial revolution also changed travel from social to business travel. There was an urge for quick and clean service because the inns were basically self-service institutions.

During the era of 1750 to 1820 the English inns gained the reputation of being the first in the world and were generally centered on London. In early England public houses were normally called "inns" or "Taverns". Normally the name Inn was reserved for finer establishments catering to the nobles while the name Taverns was awarded to the houses frequented by common man. In France the establishments were known as "Hotelleries" and the less pretentious houses called "Cabarets". The name hotel is believed to be derived from the word hotelleries around 1760. In America lodging houses were called "Inn" or "Coffee house".

By 1800 the USA were the leaders in development of first class hotels. In Swizerland Lodging houses were called "Chalets" The real growth of the modem hotels took place in the USA beginning with the opening of the "City Hotel" in 1794 in New York. This was the first building erected for hotel purpose. This period also saw the beginning of chain operations under the guidance of E. M. Statler.

Classification of Hotels

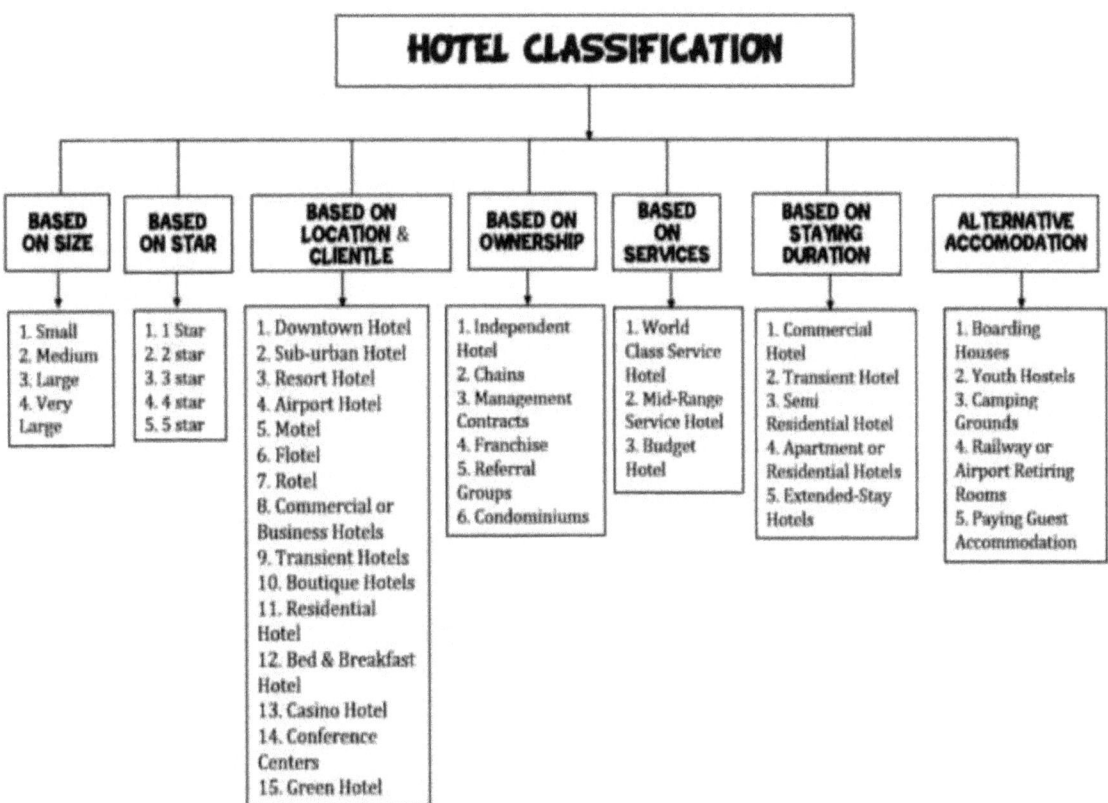

Classification of Hotels According to Types

Commercial Hotels- They have convenient locations; it primarily serves business travellers, conference groups, seminars, conventions etc. A commercial hotel also can be referred as transient hotel because of the short length of guest stay; services provided include accommodation, dinning rooms, cocktail lounges, conference halls etc. Example of such a hotel is Taj group of hotels.

1. **Airport Hotels-** It evolved because of increase in travel. Typical target markets of such hotels include airline passengers with overnight travel stay over or cancelled flights, business cliental. Example of such a hotel is Centaur at Juhu.

   This kind of hotel features guest room with living room or the parior area and separate bedroom, bar and kitchen facilities may be provided since the living quarters are complete professionals such as accountants, lawyers, and executives find suite hotels particularly attractive since they can work or entertain in any area besides their bedroom.

2. **These hotels provide long-** Term permanent accommodation mainly for single person. The minimum period of stay could be 3 to 6 months and maximum could be extended to a.

3. **Resort Hotels-** These hotels are generally located close to a mountain, island or close to the sea. They are always located away from crowded areas. Special activities provided for guest such as discotheque, golf course, water sports, horseback riding, swimming pool, tennis court etc. The atmosphere at the resort is more relaxed than the commercial hotel.

4. **Bed And Breakfast Hotels-** The owner lives in the premises and they are responsible for serving breakfast to the guest. The price for a single room is low than the other hotels. Lunch, dinner, laundry, recreational facilities are not offered.

5. **Motels-** Motel is motor hotel located along the highways. It is meant to benefit highway travellers who are required to break their journey. Facilities such as car parking, car wash, refueling station are provided. Example of such a hotel is Suman Motels.

6. **Casino Hotels-** This hotel offers gambling facilities, slot machines, blackjack, card games etc. are offered. Food and beverage operations are secondary to a casino operation.

7. **Time-Share or Condominium Hotels-** Time-share hotels have multiple owners. Here an individual purchases ownership for accommodation for specific time period; normally, ope or two weeks in a year. The size of the room is larger as compared to other hotels. Condominium hotels have only one owner where time-share may have several owners. All kitchen facilities may be provided for cooking purpose. House keeping services may or may not provided. Example of such a hotel is Mahindra time-share hotels.

8. **Conferene Hotels-** These hotels are specially designed to handle group meetings, conference and seminars. Extensive leisure facilities like golf course, indoor and outdoor games, swimming pool etc. may be provided. Secretarial assistance, language translator facilities may also be

9. Alternative Lodging Properties (Suupplymentary Accommodation)

    This includes lodges, guests houses, rest houses, camping grounds etc.

Classification of Hotels Based up on Levels of Services

These hotels are also a growing segment of the hospitality industry. These properties provide clean, comfortable, inexpensive rooms and meet the basic needs of the guest. Type of guest includes families with children, our groups, budget minded travellers etc. The number of rooms is less, staff requirement are bare minimum.

This includes modest but sufficient level of services. Type of guest include tourist, families taking advantage of special children rates, senior citizens, travel agents, co-operate groups etc. Especially restaurants and ocffee shop may be available.

3. World Class or Full Service Hotels

These hotels provide an upper scale restaurants, lounges, elaborate decors. They are suitable for top business executives, entertain celebrities, political figures and wealthy persons. Several food and beverage outlets are available to cater to the various types of cliental. Staff requirement is higher as personal attention is given to each guest.

Classification of Hotels According To Size
Hotels may be classified into four categories :
1. Under 150 rooms - Small
2. 150 - 300 rooms - Medium

3. 300 - 600 rooms - Large

4. More than 600 rooms - Very Large

Classification on The Basis of Ownership

Hotels can be categorized by ownership. There are six different ways hotels can be owned and operated

- Independently owned and operated.
- Independently owned but leased to an operator.
- Owned by a single entity or group that has hired a hotel management company to operate the property.
- Owned and operated by a chain.
- Owned by an independent investor or group and operated by a chain.
- Owned by an individual group and operated as a franchise of a chain.

An independent hotel is not connected with any established hotel company and is owned by individual or group investors. A management company contracts with hotel owners to operate their hotels. The management company may or may not have any of its own funds invested. It is usually paid by a combination of fees plus a share of revenues and profits. A hotel chain is a group of affiliated hotels.

Example: The Capitol, Bangalore, The Imperial, New Delhi

A franchise is the authorization granted by a hotel chain to an individual hotel to use the chain's trade mark, operating systems and reservation system in return for a percentage of hotel revenues plus certain other fees, such as advertising fees. A franchiser is the party granting the franchise: holiday inn worldwide is an example of franchisor. A franchisee is the parly

Franchising in the hospitality industry is a concept that allows a company to expand more rapidly by using other people's money than if it had to acquire its own financing, the company or franchisor gets certain rights: for example to use its trademark, signs, proven operating systems,operatingproceduresandpossiblereservationsystemmarketingknow-how,purchasing discounts and so on for a fee. in return the franchisee agrees by signing the franchise contract to operate the restaurant hotel and so on in accordance with the guidelines set by the franchisor. Franchising is a way of doing business that benefits both the franchisor -who wants to expand the business rapidly- and the franchisee that has a financial backing but lacks specific expertise and recognition.

The Benefits To The Franchisee Arc As Follows:

A set of plans and specifications from which to build National advertising Centralized reservation system.

Participation in volume discount in purchasing furnishings, fixtures and equipment.

The Benefits to The Franchise Company Are As Follows:
- Increased market share/recognition
- Up front fees

Example: Le Meridien, Holiday inn

There arc also referral systems. Referral systems tend to be made up of independent properties or small chains that have grouped together for common marketing purpose. Marketing consortiums or referral associations offer similar benefits to properties such as franchises, albeit at a lower cost. Hotels and motels with a referral association share a centralized reservation system and a common image, logo as well as management training and continuing training programs.

A referral group consists of a number of properties, independently owned and operated, that join under a common identity while maintaining their autonomy. They do this for one or more of the following reasons.

- To operate a reservation system.
- To publish joint brochures.
- To share advertising.
- To refer business to each other.
- To lake advantage of joint purchasing power.
- To maintain sales offices in major traffic centers.

The referral associations offer some of the same benefits as franchises, but at much lower costs a referral association may provide the independent hotel with increased visibility, marketing and buying power, without the necessity of giving up control or ownership. Hotel and motels within a referral association share a CRS and a common image, logo, or advertising slogan. The referral association publishes a membership directory, usually given away free to interested guest. In addition the referral association may offer group buying discounts to members, as well as management training and continuing education programs, hotels pay initial fee to join the referral association and an annual membership fee. Generally this fee is much less than that paid to become a member of the hotel franchise system.

Common Reservation Systems, standardized quality, joint advertising and a recognizable logo were still are the limited objectives of the most referral groups.

Chain Hotels

Hotel chains account for a large percentage of the world's hotel room inventory. Some of the world's best hotel rooms are managed by chains.

Example: Taj Group of Hotels, Itc Chain of Hotels

Star Classification

One Star

Typically smaller hotels managed by the proprietor. The hotel is often has a more personal atmosphere. It is usually located near affordable attractions, major intersections and convenient to public transportation. Furnishings and facilities arc clean but basic. Most will not a restaurant on site but are usually within walking distance to some good low priced dining.

The hotel should have at least 10 lettable bed rooms of which at least 25% should have attached bathrooms with a bathroom for every four of the remaining rooms. At least 25% of the bathrooms should have the western style WCs.

Receptions counter with a telephone and a telephone for the use of guests and visitors.

Usually denotes independent and name brand hotel chains with a reputation for offering consistent quality amenities. The hotel is usually small to medium sized and conveniently located to moderately priced attractions. The facilities typically include telephones and TVs in the bed room some hotels offer limited restaurant service. Somehow room service and bell service are not usually provided.

- The hotel should have at least 10 lettable bed rooms of Which at least 75% should have attached bathrooms and showers with a bathroom for every four of the remaining rooms.
- 25% of the rooms should have AC.
- Receptions counter with a telephone
- Telephone on each floor if the rooms do not have a telephone each.
- Supervisory staff must understand English.
- Laundry and dry cleaning services.

Example: Woodlands Hotel, Bangalore, Kamath Yatrinivas, Bangalore Three Star

Typically these hotels offer spacious accommodations that include well appointed rooms, decorated lobbies. Bell desk services are generally not available. They are often located near major express ways or business areas, convenient to shopping and moderate to high priced attractions. The hotels usually feature medium sized restaurants they typically offer breakfast through dinner. Room service availability may vary. Valet parking, fitness centers, pools are often provided.

- The hotel should have at least 20 lettable bed rooms of which all should have attached bathrooms and tubs/showers.
- At least 50% of the rooms should be AC.

- Reception and information counter, book stall, travel agency, safe deposit etc. Telephone in each room and one for the use of visitors.
- Good quality Indian and continental food.
- Senior staff must possess a good knowledge of English.

Example: Museum Inn, Bangalore, Angsana Oasis Spa & Resort, Bangalore Four Star.

Mostly large formal hotels with reception areas, front desk service, and bell desk service. The hotels are usually located near shopping, dining, and other major attractions. The level of service is well above average. And the rooms are well lit and well furnished. Restaurant dining is usually available and is having more than one choice. Some properties will offer continental breakfast and / or happy hour delicacies. Room service is usually available during most hours. Valet parking, concierge service, fitness centers, pools are. Hotel must have 25 lettable rooms and all with attache bathrooms with shower cubicle/bath tub Should have a recognized travel agency, book stall, safe deposit facilities.

Example: Taj Gateway, Bangalore, Hotel Janpath, New Delhi, St. Marks Hotel, Five Star.

These are hotels that offer only the highest level of accommodations and services. The properties offer a high degree of personal service. Although most five star hotels are large properties, sometimes the small independent (non-chain) property offers an elegant intimacy that can not be achieved in larger setting. The hotel locations can vary from the exclusive location of suburban area to heart of the city. The hotel lobbies are sumptuous, the rooms complete with stylish furnishings, and high quality linen. The amenities often include DVD players, Jacuzzis and more. The hotels feature up to three restaurants with exquisite menus. Room service is also available 24 hours a day. Fitness centers, valet parking are typically available. A concierge is also available to assist you.

- Architectural features and general construction of the hotel building should be distinctive.
- Adequate parking space for cars.
- Hotel must have at least 25 lettable; rooms with modem shower chambers.
- All guest areas should be air-conditioned.
- Adequate number of efficient lifts.
- 24 hours reception, cash and information counter.

Example: The Oberoi, Bangalore, The Grand Maratha Sheraton, Mumbai, Taj Bengal and The Park, Kolkota, The Inter-Continenetal Park Royal, New Delhi, ITC hotel Maurya Sheraton & towers, New Delhi.

Other Hotel Categories
Casino Hotels

Casino hotels and resorts differ significantly in their operation compared to most hotels. In casino hotels and resorts, gaming operations are the major revenue centers. Most of these are in Las Vegas. The casino industry is now coming into the financial main stream to the point that as a significant segment of the entertainment industry especially in the US. Casino hotels are leaning towards making their hotels into "family friendly".

They have baby sitters available at any point of the day, children's attractions ranging from parks to circuses and museums, and kid's menus in the restaurant for adults in addition to gaming health spas for relaxation, dance clubs, and dazzling shows are available.

Example: Las Vegas Hilton Hotel & Casino, MGM Grand, Flaming Hilton in Las Vegas.

Heritage Hotels

The concept of Heritage Hotels was introduced with a view to convert the old palaces, havelies, castles, forts and residences built prior to 1950 into accommodation units as these traditional structures reflect the ambience and lifestyle of the bygone era and are immensely popular with the tourists. The scheme is aimed at ensuring that such properties, landmarks of our heritage are not lost due to decay but become financially viable properties providing additional room capacity for the tourists.

The Heritage Hotels Have Also Been Sub-Classified in The Following Categories:

Heritage: This category covers hotels in residences / havelies / hunting lodges / castles / forts / palaces built prior to 1950 but after 1935.

Heritage: This category covers hotels in residences / havelies / Hunting Classic lodges / castles / forts / places built prior to 1935 but after 1920. Heritage : This category covers hotels in residences / havelies / hunting.

Grand lodges / castles / forts / palaces built prior to 1920.

Till the end of March 2002, as many as 69 properties have been classified as Heritage Hotels providing a room capacity of 1810 rooms. Guidelines have also been formulated for conversion of heritage properties into heritage hotels and their approval at project planning stage.

Example: Usha Kiran Palace, Gwalior, Lalitha Mahal Palace, Mysore.

Rambagh Palace, Jaipur, Lake Pichola hotel, Udaipur.

Time Shares/Condominiums

Time-sharing, more recently known as vacation ownership, involves a "type of shared ownership in which the buyer purchases the right to uses a residential dwelling unit for a portion of the year or more periods. Each condominium or unit of a vacation ownership resort is divided into intervals, typically by the week and sold separately. The condominiums are priced according to a variety of factors including unit size, resort amenities, location and season.

Purchasers of vacation ownership properties can typically travel to other destinations through exchange programs provided through the timeshare resort developers. Condominium hotels are also called condo hotels or even condotels. Vacation ownership offers consumers the opportunity to purchase fully furnished vacation accommodations in a variety of forms, such as weekly intervals or points in points based systems, for a percentage of the cost of the full ownership.

For a one lime purchase price and payment of a yearly maintenance fee, purchasers own their vacation either in perpetuity or for a predetermined number of years.

During the 1960s and 1970s, when inflation was a serious problem in many countries, time sharing-which first started in the French Alps in the 1960s-seemed like an idea whose.

Example: RCI, Club Mahindra, Country Club Group.

Boutique hotels span all price segments and are noticeably different in look and feel from traditional lodging properties interior design styles in boutique hotels range from postmodern to homey. Soft attributes, such and image and atmosphere, typically distinguish these properties. Traveler's desires to be trendy, affluent and artistic lie into boutique themes.

Example: The Park, Bangalore, The Park, Kolkota.

All-Suite Hotels

All suite hotels became known as a separate category in the 1970s. guest rooms are larger than the normal hotel room usually containing more than 500 square feet. A living area or parlor is typically separate from the bedroom, with some properties offering kitchen areas. All-suite hotels can be found in urban, sub-urban and even residential locations. The amenities and services can vary widely in this type of hotels.

All suite hotels were originally positioned to attract extended stay travellers, but they roved popular with other kinds of travellers as well. An all suite hotel gave guest more private space.

Example: Residence inns, Fairfield Suites & Town-Place Suites by the Marriot chain.

Convention Hotels

Convention hotels are large with 500 or more guest rooms. These properties offer extensive meeting and function space, typically including large ball rooms and even exhibition areas. Food and beverage operations tend to be extensive, with several restaurants and lounges, banquet facilities and room service. Convention hotels arc often in close proximity to convention centers and other convention hotels, providing facilities for city wide conventions and trade shows.

These hotels have many banquet areas within and around the hotel complex. These hotels have a high percentage of double occupancies. Convention hotels may also offer a concierge floor to cater to individual guest needs. Round the clock room service, an in house laundry, a business center, a travel desk, and an airport shuttle service are other amenities found in convention hotels.

Conference Hotels/Centers

Although all hotels with meeting facilities complete for conferences there arc specialized hotels that almost exclusively book conferences, executive meetings, and training seminars. While they provide most of the facilities found at the conventional hotels, conference centers are built to provide living and conference facilities without any outside distractions that might detract from hotels held in ordinary hotels.

Alternative Lodging Properties

Besides hotels, these are several other types of lodging establishments which compete for business and leisure travellers, recreational vehicle parks, campgrounds, and mobile home parks are somewhat like hotels since they involve the rental of space for overnight.

Another form of alternative lodging is the corporate lodging business very commonly known as serviced apartments. These are designed for guests wishing to slay for longer periods, some times up to six mouths or longer. While hotels are usually designed for guests staying from one to ten nights, corporate lodging is better suited to guests with very long slay requirements. Instead of using hotels or hotel buildings, corporate lodging usually provides fully furnished apartments for guests. The service provider rents the apartment, provides furniture and house wares, and provides housekeeping and other services to the guests. Corporate lodging is usually cost competitive with hotels, since apartments can be rented and furnished by the owner or the service provide for a lower daily cost than that incurred by hotels.

Example: Slay and Work, Bangalore.

Another example of alternative lodging is the cruise ship industry. Cruise ships have become major competition for resorts. They offer many amenities offered similarly at island resorts, while having the unique advantage of moving from island to island as part of the experience. Modem cruise ships offer all the advantages of resort hotels they are equipped with many modem convenience such as ship to shore telephones, satellite television, fitness centers, movie theaters, multiple dining and cocktail lounge facilities, spas, casinos, shopping, and of course no Velty to waking up in different location at every morning. Some cruise ships now even offer conference facilities for corporate or association meetings.

Example: Carnival Cruise liners, Caribbean Cruise liners, Norwegian cruise liners.

Front Desk Layoutand Equipment

LOBBY LAYOUT

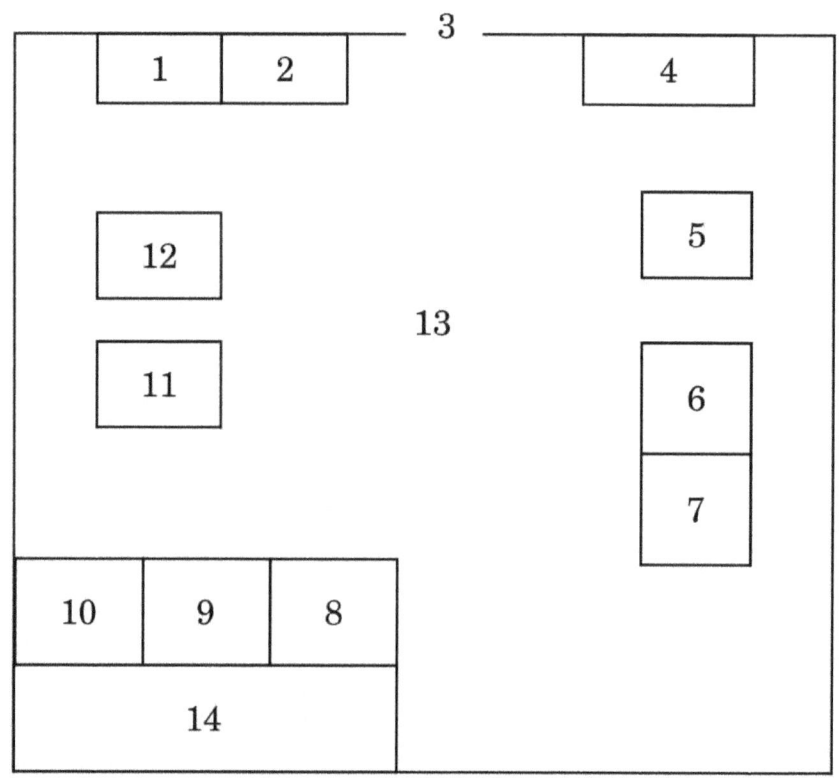

Keys:

1. Left Luggage Counter.
2. Bell Desk.
3. Entrance.
4. Travel Desk.
5. Lobby Manager.
6. House Phone.
7. Public Phone.
8. Reception.

9. Information.
10. Cashier.
11. Counter for Group and Crew Arrivals.
12. Guest Relation Executive Counter.
13. Lobby.
14. Back Area or Back Office.

Front Office Equipment

1. Mail, Message and Key Rack

A key rack is an array of numbered compartments used to store guest room keys. Key rack used to be visible to individuals both behind and in front of the desk.

To minimize a number of racks in front desk area hotels may combine the key rack with either the room rack or the mail and message rack.

A combination of mail, message and key rack can be either a freestanding wall unit or an under the counter row of compartments.

2. Folio Rack

In non-automated and semi automated purposes guest folios are stored in a front office folio tray and arranged by guest room numbers. Guest room folios remain in the tray throughout the occupancy of the guest cycle, except when they are used in

3. Account Posting Machine

Semi automated hotel that allow the guest to charge purchases to their room used an account-posting machine to post, monitor and balance these charges. A posting

 i. A standardize means of recording transactions.

 ii. A basis for cash and default payments management

 iii. A analysis of departmental sales activity.

 iv. An audit tray of charges, purchases transactions.

4. Telephone

EPABX: Electronic Private Automatic Branch Exchange.

5. Fax Facsimile

6. Credit Card Investors

An imprinter presses a credit card voucher against a guest credit card. The impact causes the raised credit card number, expiry date, name of the cardholder to the recorded on the voucher for use in credit card billing and collection procedure.

7. Magnetic Strip Reader

It reads data magnetically recorded and stored in the magnetic tape. The strip on the back of a credit card transmits the data to a credit card verification service on basis of the credit card data and transaction data, the credit card verification service either approves or disapproves the transaction.

8. Time Stand
Folios, mails and other front office paper work are inserted into a time stand device to record the correct time and date.

9. Wake Up Device
The non-automated wake up device is usually a special designed clock with multiple alarms setting to remain. Front office agent or telephone operator place wake up calls.

10. Security Monitor
Close circuit television monitors allow front office or security personnel to monitor a certain area of hotel from a central location.

Front Officer Organization

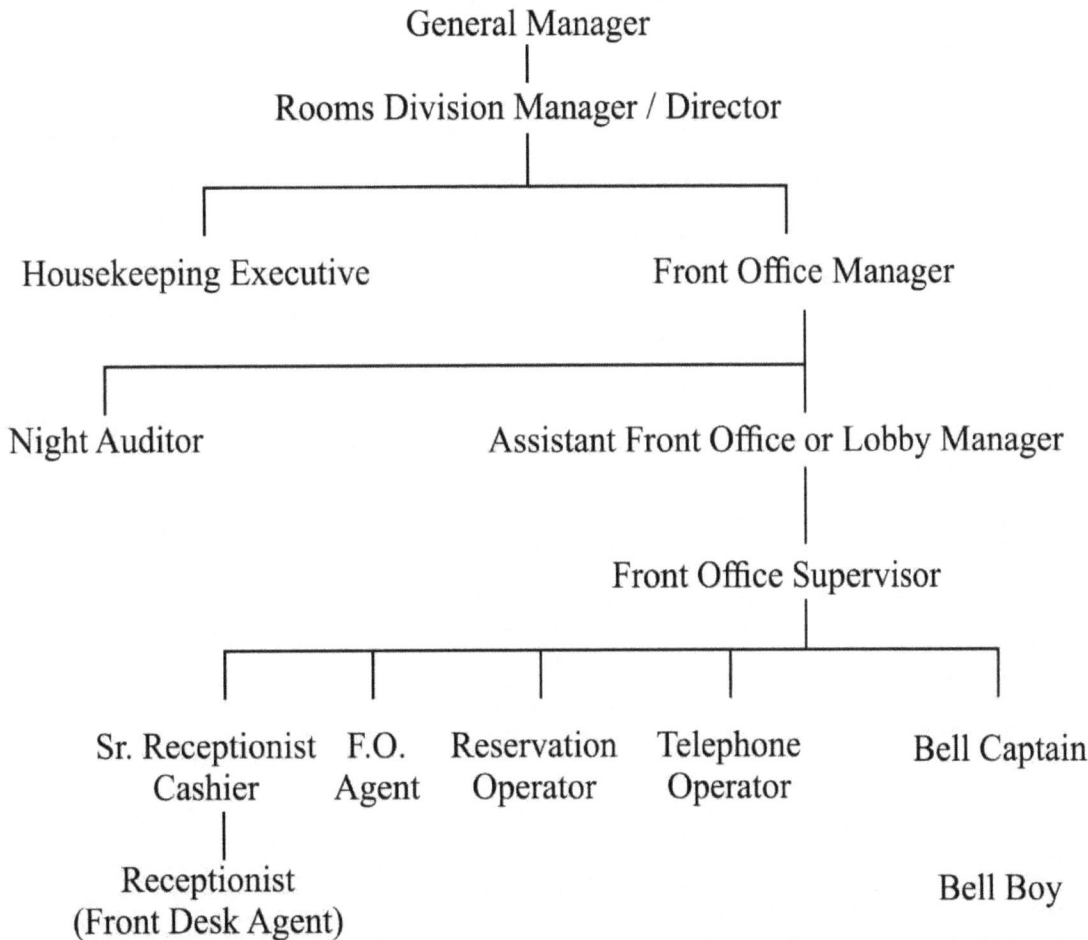

Job Description of Front Office Staffs

Job Description	Front Office Manager.
Job Title	Front Office Manager.
Reports To	General Manager.

Duties And Responsibilities:
1. Participate in the selection of front office personnel.
2. Train, cross train and re-train all front office personnel.

3. Schedule the front office staff.
4. Supervise workload during shifts.
5. Evaluate the job performance of front office employees.
6. Maintain working relationship and communicate with all departments.
7. Maintain master key control.
8. Verify that accurate room status information is maintained and properly communicated.
9. Resolve guest problem quickly, efficiently and courteously.
10. Update group information, maintain, monitor and prepare group requirement. Relay to appropriate personnel.
11. Review and complete credit limit report.
12. Work within the allocated budget for front office.
13. Review information from the previous shift managers and pass on details to the on coming managers.
14. Check cashiers in and out and verify balance and deposits at the end of the shift.
15. Enforcing all cash handling, cheque handlings and credit policies.
16. Conduct regularly scheduled meetings of the front office personnel.

Reports To: Lobby Manager or Assistant Front Office Manager

1. Process reservation by mail, telephone, telex, fax or by central reservation system.
2. Process reservation from the sales office, other hotel departments and travel agents.
3. Know the type of rooms available as well as their locations and layouts.
4. Know the selling status, rates and benefits of all package plans.
5. Know the credit policy of the hotel and how to code each reservation.
6. Create and maintain reservation records by date of arrival in alphabetical order.
7. Determine room rates based on the selling tactics of the hotel.
8. Prepare letter of confirmation.
9. Communicate reservation information to the front desk.
10. Process cancellations and modifications. Promptly relay this information to the front desk.
11. Understand the hotels policy on guaranteed reservations and no shows.
12. Process advance deposits on reservations.
13. Track future room availability on basis of reservations.
14. Help develop room revenue and occupancy report.
15. Prepare expected arrival list for front office use.
16. Assist in pre-registration activities when appropriate.
17. Monitor advance deposit requirement.
18. Handle daily correspondence: respond to enquiries and make reservations as needed.
19. Make sure that files arc kept up to date.

Job Description	Telephone Operator.
Job Title	Telephone Operator,
Reports To	Lobby Manager or Assistant Front office Manager.

Duties And Responsibilities:

1. Answers incoming calls.
2. Directs calls to guest rooms, staff or departments through a PBX system.
   - **EPBX:** Electronic Private Branch Exchange.
3. Receive telephone charges from telephone companies and forwards charges to
4. Take and distribute messages from guest.
5. Log all wake up call requests and perform wake up call service.
6. Provide information about guest services to guest
7. Answer questions about hotel events and activities.
8. Know what action to be taken when an emergency call is requested or received.

Job Description	Front Office Cashier.
Job Title	Front Office Cashier.
Reports To	Assistant Front office Manager or Lobby Manager.

Duties And Responsibilities:

1. Operates front office posting equipment.
2. Obtains the house bank and keeps it balanced.
3. Complete cashiers pre-shift supply checklist.
4. Takes departmental reading at the beginning of the shift.
5. Complete guest check in procedures.
6. Post charges to guest account
7. Handle pay out vouchers.
8. Cash guest cheques.
9. Complete checkout procedures.
10. Settle guest accounts.
11. Handle cash, traveler's cheque, personal cheque, credit card and direct billing request properly.
12. Transfer folios paid by credit card to each credit cards master file.

13. Transfer folio charges to the non-guest ledger to each company's master file.
14. Balance departmental totals at the close of shift.
15. Manage safe deposit lockers.

Job Description	Receptionist
Job Title	Receptionist

Reports To : Assistant Profit Office Manager or Lobby Manager.

1. Receive guest with a smile and answering queries of new arrivals and providing correct information. Efficient handling of new arrivals with allocation of rooms with delays, helping and guiding in filling of registration form.
2. The receptionist handle walk in. regular guest who arrive without reservation, she
3. Allocation of rooms to group in co-ordination with the tour co-coordinator.
4. Checks the house keeping reports with room status reports land see's that are no
5. Know the location of the rooms and decor.

Job Description	Bell Captain.
Job Title	Bell Captain.
Reports To	Lobby Manager or Assistant Front Office Manager.

Duties And Responsibilities:

1. He is responsible to the lobby manager for the conduct appearance and work performance of the bellboys.
2. He controls the movement of bellboys.
3. He fixes their duty router and allocates work accordingly.
4. He checks with the reception about scanty baggage. He reports irregularities of suspicious persons to the lobby manager on duty.
5. He prepares errand cards for the bellboys.

Job Description	Bellboy.
Job Title	Bellboy.
Reports To	Bell Captain.

Duties And Responsibilities:

1. He is accountable for his actions to the bell captain.
2. He carries luggage, parcels etc. to guest room. He shows the guest around the room.

3. He should posses through knowledge about the topography of the hotel.
4. He distributes mails to various departments as well as guest.
5. He distributes newspapers to the guest.
6. He should be familiar with luggage, storage procedures and luggage room.
7. He keeps postage stamps available for guest request
8. He sees that the C-Form is deposited to the nearest police station or the registration

The Guest Cycle

The guest cycle suggests a systematic approach to managing front office operations. The four stages of the guest cycle are as follows.

1. Pre-Arrival

The guest chooses a hotel during this stage. The guest's choice can be affected by many factors including previous experiences with the hotel, advertisements, recommendations from he travel agents, friends or business associates. This decision may also be influenced by the ease of making reservations and how the reservation agent describes the hotel and its facilities, room rates and amenities. The attitude, efficiency of the front office staff may influence a caller's decision to stay at a particular hotel. A reservation agent must be able to respond quickly and accurately to requests for future accommodation. If a reservation can be accepted as requested, the reservation agent creates a reservation record. The creation of a reservation record initiates the hotel guest cycle. This record enables the hotel to personalize guest service and schedule needed staff and fa< lities. By confirming a reservation, the hotel verifies a guest's room request and personal information and assures the guest that his or her needs will be addressed. Because of information collected, the hotel may also be able to perform pre-registration. Such activities include assigning a specific room and rate for guest who have not yet arrived and creating guest folios.

The arrival stage of the guest cycle includes registration and rooming functions. When the guest arrives at the hotel, he or she establishes a business relationship with the hotel through the front office staff. The front office desk agent should determine the guest's reservation status before beginning the registration process. Guests without reservation or the walk in guests, present an opportunity for front desk agents to sell guestrooms.

To sell successfully, the front desk agents must be very familiar with the hotel room types and guest services and be able to describe them in a positive way. A guest will not register if he or she is not convinced of the value of renting a particular hotel room. A registration record should include information about the guest's intended method of payment, the planned length of stay, special requests such as a rollaway bed or particular room location. It should also include the guest's telephone number, address and signature. Obtaining the guest's signature is a very important part of the registration process. Front desk agents must possess knowledge about the difference in amenities provided in all rooms. New properties coming up should be barrier-free in design. This means that facilities and accommodation must be designed with the disabled in mind. Some of the features of barrier-free guestrooms include extra wide doors for wheelchairs, extra large bathrooms; grab bars at the toilet and in the bath, low vanity counter tops. Once the guest decides to rent a room, the front desk agent turns his attention to identifying the guest's method of payment, the front office should take measures at the beginning of the guest cycle to ensure eventual payment. Registration is complete once methods of payment and the guest's departure date have been established. The guest may be given the room key and the bellboy may be asked to show the guest to his room. When the guest arrives at the room and accepts it, the occupancy stage of the guest cycle begins.

2. Occupancy

The manner in which the front office staff represents the hotel is important throughout the guest cycle, particularly during the occupancy stage. The front office should respond to requests in a timely and accurate way to maximize guest satisfaction. The front office staff must encourage repeat visits. Front desk agents should carefully attend to complaints and try to find satisfactory solutions. Front desk accounting records must be periodically reviewed for accuracy and completeness.

The final element of guest service is checking the guest out of the hotel and creating a guest history record. At check out, the guest vacates the room, receives an accurate statement of account for settlement, returns the room keys and departs from the hotel. Once the guest has checked out, the front office updates the room availability status and notifies the housekeeping department During check out the front office determines whether the guest was satisfied with the stay and encourages the guest to return to the hotel in the future. The more information the hotel has about its guests, the better it can serve their needs and develop marketing strategies to increase business. Once the guest has checked out, the front office can analyze data related to the guest's stay. Front office reports can be used to review operations, isolate problem areas, indicate where corrective action may be needed and point out business trends. Analysis can help managers establish a standard of performance, which can be used to evaluate the effectiveness of the front office operations.

Types of Rooms

1. Single Room
It is a room, which consists of single bed and has a capacity for one persons.

2. Double Bed Room
It is a room, which consists of double bed and has capacity for two persons.

3. Quad Room
This room has capacity to provide accommodation for four persons with two double beds.

4. Twin Room
This room has two single beds separated by a side table and has a separates headboard.

This room has two single beds to provide accommodation for two persons, which is separated by a side table and has a common headboard.

This room has separate dinning, sitting room, which are partitioned using temporary.

Two rooms attached with a common door, which is meant for families.

Two rooms with a common wall but no common door.

5. Studio Rooms
A room, which consists of a sofa cum bed.

6. Cabana
A room, which is situated near the swimming pool car on the same level of that, of the pool.

7. Duplex Rooms
Rooms with staircase within the room area like split-levels.

8. Senior Rooms
They are rooms, which have a separate dinning, sitting room, and a bedroom separated by walls.

9. Pent-house Suite
It is a room bn the top most floors, which has an open terrace. A room which is similar to penthouse suite but with additional facilities and fittings is Presidential Suite.

Rate Categories

1. Food Plans

1. European Plan (E.P)
This plan includes room rates and early morning tea.

2. Continental Plan (C. P)
This plan includes room rates and continental breakfast.

3. Bermuda Plan (B.P)
This plan includes room rates and American breakfast.

This plan includes room rates, English breakfast, lunch and dinner.

This plan includes room rates, English breakfast and either lunch or dinner.

Corporate travellers receive preferential treatment as the "bread and butter" clientele of the typical commercial logging establishing. A corporate rate program encourages business from employees traveling on the behalf of the participating company. To earn a corporate discount, the company may have be required to guarantee a minimum number of rooms to be occupied during a set period of time.

2. Agent Rate
The agent rate is the hotel's discounted rate for the travel agents and airline personnel. An agent rate is generally not valid during periods when the hotel is sold out.

3. Packaged Rate
The hotel's package rate usually include promotional discounts to encourages occupancy during slack or off-season periods, or to introduce new prospective to the facilities. The following types of rate package are examples:

Weekend Rate: A commercial hotel, which relies heavily on the business travellers typically, has a low occupancy rate on weekends. A special weekend rate may apply for weekend packages - usually Friday, Saturday and Sunday nights. This package may include a food and beverage allowance at the hotel's restaurant.

Promotional Package Rate: Resorts hotels with strong weekend and holiday business often experience low occupancy during the week. To boost occupancy levels during these slack periods, the hotel may offer a promotional package rate, normally based on the double occupancy for the stays of three days to one week. The package may include a food and beverage at the hotel's restaurant, or such amenities as free gambling chips at the hotel casino.

Basis of Charging

Here a day of stay is calculated from 12 noon to 12 noon of the following day. Number of nights spent at the property. Hotels do not entertain this but small inns.

Here a day of stay is calculated on 24 hours basis.

Front Office Systems

Semi-Automated System

A semi-automated system or electro-mechanical, front office system depends on both handwritten and machine produced forms. Advantages of a. semi-automated system over a non-automated system included automatically generated and easy to read documents that detailed the steps of a transaction these documents represented what is known as an audit trail. The disadvantages of semi-automated equipment included the complexities of operating and controlling devices that were not integrated with other systems and that were subject to frequent maintenance problems.

Pre-Arrival Activities: Guests making reservations would call a national reservations network or contact the hotel directly. When reservation requests grew beyond the front desk's ability to handle them efficiently, many hotels created a reservation department. Pre-registration activities included preparation of registration cards (Reg-cards), guest folios and information slips. Room assignments were usually made based on room rack status, as in a non-automated process. As in non-automated hotels, semi-automated properties usually opted to maintain a manual reservation density board.

Arrival Activities: When guests with reservations arrived at the hotel, they simply verified the previously recorded registration information and signed a preprinted registration card. Walk-in guests generally completed a multiple-copy registration card. Copies were distributed to (he room rack, the switch board operator and the information rack.

Occupancy Activities: The use of semi-automated systems did not significantly reduce the paperwork needed to chart the guest cycle. Vouchers were used to communicate charge purchases to the front desk, and revenue outlets relied on sales record entries to prove transactions. Mechanical and electronic cash registers and front office posting machines were used to process many of the records formerly processed by hand. The use of this equipment enabled the front office to handle guest accounting transactions more accurately and rapidly. A night audit procedure based on posting machine records was used to verify account entries and balances.

Departure Activities: A more through audit routine, made possible by a semi-automated system, led to faster and smoother guest check-outs. Front desk agents experienced fewer discrepancies in guest accounts and were able to efficiently reconcile guest accounts.

They were also able to relay room status information to house-keeping much more quickly than they could in a non-automated system. Registration cards were collected and placed in the property's guest history file for future reference.

Fully-Automated System or Property Management Systems

Front office record keeping in a computer based property management system is mostly the result of programmed routines. Computer systems designed for use in the hospitality industry were first introduced in early 1970s, but were not considered viable until the late 1970s. During 1980s computer equipments became less expensive, more compact and easier to operate. Intellect data system (IDS). Fidelio is some of the popular PMS used in our industry.

Pre-Arrival Activities: The reservation software of an in-house PMS may directly interface with a central Reservation system(CRS) or Global distribution System (GDS) and automatically quote rates and reserve rooms according to a predetermined pattern. The reservation software may also automatically generate letters of confirmation, produce request for guest deposits, handle pre-registration activities and establish credit status of the traveler if a credit card or debit card.

Number has been provided at the time the reservation is made. Electronic folios can be established and pre-registration transactions can be processed for guests with confirmed reservations. A reservation software package may also generate an expected arrivals list, occupancy and revenue forecasts and a variety of informative reports.

Arrival Activities: Guest information collected during reservation process is automatically transferred from the computer's reservation record to the front office software of the PMS. For walk-in guests, guest information is entered in to the front office system by a front desk agent. The agent may then present a computer prepared registration card to the guest for verification and signature. The installation of on-line credit card authorization terminals helps front desk personnel to receive timely credit card approval. Registration data, stored electronically the system, can be retrieved whenever necessary, thereby making a room rack unnecessary. Electronic guest folios are also maintained and accessed through

Self Check-in

In addition, some properties offer self check-in/check-out terminals. In fact these terminals have been in existence for many years, but only recently has the cost of the technology been significantly reduced.

In addition, the acceptance of automated teller machines (ATM) used by most banks and self check-in terminals at airports has had a direct impact on guests who are willing to accept self-help equipments in lodging establishments.

To use one of these terminals the guest inserts a credit card, debit card or smart card in to the machine, which reads encoded card data and communicates with the property management system. The central system locates the guest's reservation and returns the information to the terminal. The guest is asked to verify name, departure date, and rate and room type on the display. Some system allow changes to this information and some require that the guest go to the front desk for amendment (changes). If the information is correct the system assigns an available room within the PMS and dispenses a rooming slip to different departments and issues guest room keys. Advanced systems provide electronic room keys that are individually created when the guest checks in.

Occupancy Activities: With a front office system, on-automated room racks and electromechanical or electro posting machines are replaced by computer terminals throughout the front office. As guests charge purchases at revenue outlets, the charged amounts are electronically transferred to the front office computer from the POS (point of sale) location. These charges are then automatically posted to the proper electronic guest folio, instantaneous postings, simultaneous guest accounts and departmental entries and continuous trial balances free the front office auditor to spend time on auditing rather than focusing primarily on guest account balancing.

Departure Activities: A Neatly printed electronic folio helps assure the guest that the statement is complete end accurate. Depending on the method of settlement, the computer system may automatically post the transaction to appropriate back office accounts. For a guest account that requires third-party billing, the system is capable of producing a bill to be sent to the guest or credit granting agency. Once the guest's account is settled and the postings arc considered complete, departed guest information is used to create an electronic record in the hotel's guest history file.

Property Management System

Property management system contains assets of computer software package capable of supporting a variety of activities in front office and bask office areas. The four most common front office software package are designed to assist front office employees perform functions related to

1. Reservation Management
2. Room Management
3. Guest Account Management
4. General Management

1. Reservation Management Software

A computer based reservation package enables & hotel to rapidly process room request and generate timely and accurate rooms, revenue and forecasting reports. Most lodging chains participate in computer based central reservation system.

Central reservation- system typically stores the reservation data, track room reserve, control reservation by room type and room rate and monitor the number of reservation.

Reservation received at a central reservation office can be processed, confirmed and communicated to the destination property. The most modem system allows two-way communication between central reservation office and hotel computers. This way accurate hotel guest room inventories and pricing are provided to both systems.

Various reservation management reports containing summary of reservation date and guest account status information can be generated. Current reservation management software also includes upgraded room control feature, guest history module and more detailed property information such as bed types, guest room view and special features.

2. Room Management Software

Room management software maintains current information on the status of rooms, provides information on room rates, assists in room assignment during registration and help front office personnel co-ordinate pest services.

A room management module can also be used to provide rapid access to room availability date during the reservation process. This information can be especially useful in short-term reservation confirmation and room revenue forecasting. Room management software can provide front desk employees with a summary of each room status just as the room rack and information rack does in a non-automated and semi-automated hotels.

In the computerized system, the front office employee simply enters the room number at a computer system terminal and the current status of the room appears immediately on the terminals display screen.

Once the room has been cleaned and ready for occupancy, the house keeping staff can communicate the room status by means of a terminal located in the housekeeping department or in some case through a telephone interface. With a computerized system changes in the room status are communicated to the front desk. In addition, front desk agent can enter a guest specific request into the computer to find a room that exactly needs his or her needs.

3. Guest Account Management Software

Guest account management software increases the hotels control over guest account and significantly modifies the traditional night audit routine. Quest accounts are maintained electronically thereby eliminating much of the need for folio cards, folio tray and account posting machine. The guest accounting module monitors pre-determine guest credit limit and provides flexibility through multiple folio format. At checkout previously approved outstanding account balances can be automatically transferred to an appropriate account receivable file for a subsequent billing and collection.

When the hotels revenue outlets are connected to the front office computer system, the remote cash register can be used to communicate guest charges to the front office. These charges can then be automatically posted to appropriate guest folios. This helps reduce late charges posted to guest account after the guest has departed.

4. General Management

General management software cannot operate independently of other front office software packages. General management applications tend to be report generating packages which depend on data collected through reservation management, room management and guest account management programs. For example, general management software may be able to generate a report showing the days expected arrival and the number of rooms available for occupancy: a combination of reservation and room management data. In addition to generating reports, the general management module serves as a central link between front and back office computer system interface application.

Back Office Interface

A comprehensive property management system typically involves the hotels back office. Although front and back offices software packages can be implemented independently of each other, integrated system offer the hotel a full range of control over a variety of operational areas. Such areas include room sales, telephone call accounting, payroll and account analysis. An integrated system cannot produce complete financial statement unless all the required data are stored in the systems memory. Many reports generated by the back office system depend on the front office system collection of data. The four most popular applications are :

1. Account receivable software, which monitors guest account and account billing and collection when integrated with the front office guest accounting module.

2. Account payable application, which tracks the hotels purchases and helps the hotel maintain sufficient cash flow to satisfy its debts.

3. Payroll accounting application, which processes such data as time and attendance record, pay distribution and tax with holdings.
4. Financial reporting operation, which helps the hotel develop a chart of accounts in order to produce balance sheets, income statement and transactional analysis reports.

Front Office Interface

A variety of front office interface applications are available to a fully automated logic properties.

1. Non-Guest Operated Interface

Some interfaces that are not operated by guest include:

i. A point of sale system, which allows guest account transaction to be quickly transmitted from remote point of sale to the front desk for automatic account folio.

ii. A call accounting system, which directs, prices and tracks guestroom telephone use.

iii. Electronic, locking system, which may interface with the room management application to provide enhanced guest security.

iv. A credit card settlement system, which can capture verify and authorize credit card information and settlement account

2. Guest Operated Interface

More and more hotels may provide computerized conveniences and services. Some hotels have gone beyond basic property management system by installing a variety of automated devices that can be operated by guest. In some properties guest may inquire about in-house events and local activities through automated information devices in public areas.

There are two types of in room beverage service system. Non-automated honor bars are stocked of beverage items in both dry and cold storage areas within a guest room. The bars beginning inventory level is recorded and changes in the inventory arc noted by the hotel employees on a daily bases. Appropriate charges are posted to guest folio.

Fully automated guestroom, vending machines contain electro optical sensors that record the removal of stored products from designated compartments. When a sensor is triggered, the vending machine sends appropriate information to the front office accounting module for folio posting.

Reservation

Reservation is the process of booking and blocking of rooms for the future. The most important outcome of the reservation process is having a guest room ready and waiting when the guest arrives. This guest room should not be just any room but the room that best meets the needs the guest expressed during the reservation process.

Processing reservations involves matching room requests with room availability, recording, confirming and maintaining reservations and producing management reports. Reservation information is especially useful in other front office functions. For example: with the information gathered during the reservation process, front office personnel can finalize room rate assignment and create account and guest history file.

Sources of Reservations

The travel agent operates in the local market He may receive request from the tour organizer to plan itineraries both for individuals and groups in his country or region. In short they put all the elements of the infrastructure together into one package.

They organize packages in which the stay is inclusive so they themselves make hotel reservations for their clients. They are different from travel agents in respect that they make reservations in large numbers.

They make reservations to accommodate their company delegates, business associates. They make reservations for presentations, seminars etc. The company sends a letter of reservation to the hotel, the accounts department at the hotel then verifies the credits of the company and accordingly confirms and sends the confirmation letter to the company. Then the company issues the letter to their delegates or associates. This letter is produced at the reception counter when the guest of the company arrives at the hotel.

1. Individuals
   i. Walk in.
   ii. Free Individual Traveler (FIT)
   iii. Free Foreign Individual Traveler (FFIT)

2. Embassies
They make reservations when they have their delegates, counselors, ambassadors and head of state visiting.

3. Airlines
They make room reservations when they have to give accommodation to their crew and passengers when there are flight cancellations or long flight delays. The airline also makes

reservation for their passengers during transit stay, as there is a long time (at least 6 hours) during the connected flights.

4. Tourist Office

They make room reservation but only of hotels or inns, which belong to the government. Every state has a tourist office to make reservations convenient to the local people as well as tourist

5. Government Agencies

They make reservations whenever there are state organized cultural activities, programs, functions or sports events. These agencies make reservations to accommodate their delegates, distinguished guest, VIP's, WIP's, the participants of

This happens when the hotel cannot accommodate a walk in client or a group in their own property, but wants to develop a relation and goodwill with this group or individual.

6. Central Reservation Office (C. R. O.)

This is done when it is chain of hotels. They make reservations for their clients in any state the client will be proceeding or traveling, provided they have their property in that particular state where the client is heading or intending to travel.

Taxi drivers, rickshaw drivers, local guides etc.

Mode or Medium of Reservations
Mode of Reservation

Written	Visual
Fax	Internet
Telegram	Email
Letter	CRS

Written

1. **Fax**

   Advantage: On spot reservation and confirmation cart be done.

   Disadvantage: It is expensive.

Verbal or Oral

Telephones Counter / Walk in

2. **Telegram**

   Disadvantage: Very limited information can be sent.

3. **Letter**

   Advantage: It is convenient, cheap and one could really make himself or herself very clear.

   Disadvantage: Though so popular there is always a fear that it might not reach in Time or might not reach at all.

Visual

1. **Internet**

   Advantage: It is then and there, easiest, convenient.

   Disadvantage: One requires a computer and a phone line. Phone line could be seen to be cheap but a computer could be said to be expensive, even if cyber cafe is used to access Internet, not all could afford it.

   Advantage: it is fastest and convenient

   Disadvantage: One requires a computer and a phone line. Phone line could be seen to be cheap but a computer could be said to be expensive, even if cyber cafe is used to access Internet and e-mailing, not all could afford it.

2. **Central Reservation System (C. R. S)**

   Advantage: One point of accessing information, easy and very convenient.

   Disadvantage: The set up and maintenance cost is very high.

   Advantage: It is the shortest and the best way.

   Disadvantage: It is not expensive and affordable if it is a local call, it is a bit expensive if it is a national call and it is very expensive if it is an international call.

3. **Counter or Walk in**

   Advantage: It is face-to-face and straight.

   Disadvantage: The words if misunderstood may put one in uncomfortable situation. Sometimes language also becomes a problem.

Activities Associated with The Reservation Process

The activities associated with the reservation process are:

1. Conducting the Reservation Enquiry

A property can receive reservations in many ways. Reservation requests may be made in person, over the telephone, through mail, through a central reservation system. Regardless of the source, the reservation agent will collect the following information about the guest stay through a process known as reservation enquiry. The agent will ask for such information as the guest name, address, telephone number, company or travel name, date of arrival and departure, type and number of rooms requested. The agent will also clarify the room rate, number of people in the party, method of payment or guarantee, any special requests.

Most of the information gathered through the enquiry process will be used to create the reservation record. The reservation agent enters the gathered information onto a reservation form or onto a computer terminal according to clearly defined procedures.

Reservations can be made for individuals, groups, tours or conventions. For groups, reservation may be filed under the group name rather than individual names.

2. Reservation Availability

When a property receives a reservation enquiry, it is important to compare the data with previously processed reservations. Processing a reservation results in one of

   i. Accept the reservation as requested.
   ii. Suggest alternative room types, dates and rates.
   iii. Suggest alternative hotel properties.

In any reservation system, it is necessary to closely monitor the number of reservations in order to avoid overbooking. A hotel should use care when accepting reservations after all its rooms are occupied or reserved. A hotel may strive to book every room to achieve a full house. Experienced reservation managers forecast their cancellation and no show. Then they book the hotel slightly beyond its actual capacity to assure that as many rooms are occupied as possible. Overbooking should be approached cautiously. If a reservation manager books too many rooms, guests with confirmed reservations may have to be turned away. This creates poor guest relations and discourages repeat business. Some kind of wall charts or computerized system must be maintained to monitor room availability. Computerized reservation system can tightly control room availability data and automatically generate many reservation related reports. Once all rooms in the specific category are sold, the computer can be programmed to refuse to any further reservations in that category. Some systems will automatically suggest alternative room types or rates or even other nearby hotel properties. Systems may also display open, closed and special event dates for an extended period of time. Open dates refer to available room days, while closed dates depict full house forecasts. Special event dates can be programmed to chart reservations agent that a convention or large group is expected to occupy the hotel. The future frame for tracking reservations is called the reservation horizon. Most computer-based systems have horizons of two to five years.

3. Creating Reservation Record

Reservation records identify guest and their occupancy needs before the guest actually arrive. These records enable the hotel to personalize guest service and accurately schedule staff. Reservation agent creates reservation record based on interactions with the guest These records initiate the guest cycle. However, reservation agent can create these reports only after determining that a request for a reservation can be met To create a reservation record, the reservation agent collects and enters such guest data as :

   i. Guest name.
   ii. Home address.
   iii. Telephone number and area code.
   iv. Name, address, telephone number of the guest's company if appropriate.
   v. Name of the person making reservations, if not the guests.
   vi. Number of people in the party.
   vii. Expected date and time of arrival.

viii. Reservation type, (guaranteed, non-guaranteed).

ix. Special requirements (infant, no smoking accommodation, ramp for wheel chair).

x. Additional information like method of transportation, flight number, room preference.

Reservation agents need to obtain additional information for guaranteed reservations.

Depending on the method of guarantee, an agent may be required to obtain;

1. Credit Card Information

This information consists of the credit card type, expiration date and cardholder's name. A stop list should be consulted to check if any numbers have been listed as invalid.

2. Prepayment or Deposit Information

This information comes in the form of an agreement from the guest or client that he or she will submit a required deposit to the hotel before a specified date. If this amount is not paid, the reservation may need to be cancelled or reclassified as non-guaranteed.

3. Corporate or Travel Agency Account Information

This information includes the name and address of the booking company, the name of the person making the reservation. For efficiency, the hotel may provide reservation agents with an approved list of corporate and travel agency account numbers to use for verification purposes. Individual properties and chains may defer in their policies on quoting and confirming room rates during the creation of a reservation record. Although published rates may be subject to change without notice, a rate quoted and confirmed during the reservation process must be honored. Reservation agent should be aware of several factors when quoting rates during reservation recording process including

i. Supplementary charges for extra services or amenities.

ii. Special promotions in effect for the dates requested.

iii. Applicable foreign currency exchange rates, if quoting rates to a foreign guest.

iv. Applicable room tax percentages and service charges.

4. Confirming The Reservation Record

A reservation confirmation means that the hotel acknowledged and verified a guest's room request and personal information by telephoning or mailing a letter of confirmation. A written confirmation states the intent of both parties and confirms important points of agreement, names, dates, rate, type of accommodation and number of guests. Guests arc often asked to produce a copy of the letter of confirmation at registration.

Confirmation Letters Generally Include:

- Name and address of the guest.

5. Maintaining The Reservation Records

An agent's efficiency at organizing and retrieving reservation records and related files is vital to the reservation process. If a person contacts the hotel to change a reservation, for example, the reservation agent must be able to quickly access the correct record, verify its contents and process the modification. The agent must be able to promptly re-file the reservation record and update pertinent reservation reports.

6. Producing Reservation Reports

An effective reservation system helps maximize room sales by accurately monitoring room availabilities and forecasting rooms revenue. Common management reports include:

i. Reservation Transaction Report

This report summarizes daily reservation activity in terms of reservation record creation, modification and cancellation. Other possible reports include specialized summaries such as cancellation reports, blocked room reports, no show reports.

ii. Commission Agent Report

Agents with contractual agreements may be owed commission for business they have booked at the property. This report tracks the amount owed to each agent.

iii. Turn Away Report

They report tracks the number of request refused by the hotel because rooms were not available for the requested days.

iv. Revenue Forecast Report

This report projects future revenue by multiplying predicted occupancies by current room rates. This information can be especially important for long-range planning and cash management strategies.

v. Expected Arrival And Departure Lists

Expected arrival and departure lists are prepared daily to indicate the number and names of guest expected to arrive, depart and stay over.

Room Status Board

A room status system is simply a development of the room board. Although some of the components are interchangeable with the advance reservation rack system, they do not have to use together. There is a rack for ail the rooms of the hotel with a slot for each room. The rack is tailor made for each hotel. In some system there is a Perspex (a transparent thermoplastic acrylic resin) slider which can be in one of the three positions related to the color clear, red or yellow. The room type is shown in the center of each slot, and the room types are color coded over the room number on the left. In his way the room type can be identified even when a rack slip is in place. Arrows are used to show communicating rooms. The center section can also be used to show rate and the location of each room.

The three color of Perspex slider can be used to show the current state of the room.

The advantage of room status board such as this is that more than one receptionist can register guests and allocate rooms instantly, minimizing the risk of two people being.

Electronic Room Status Board

Large hotels often install system that link reception, housekeeping and the cashier's office for automatic transfer of room status. In each of these departments an electronic board is situated, and colored bulbs denote the status of the room. It is possible to see from the color code not only which rooms are occupied or ready, but also to see which rooms currently being serviced, and therefore likely to be returned shortly.

Whitney System

Another approach was pioneered by the American Whitney Corporation. It is known as Whitney System. The Whitney System was very widely used, especially in American or American-influenced hotels. It was particularly common in large and busy hotels, and has consequently tended to be superseded by computer. However, it is still likely to be found acting as a backup manual system in such system.

The system is based on the use of standard sized cards. These can be colored coded to show various kinds of reservation (group, airlines, VIP). It is possible to obtain sets of slips made of NCR ('No Carbon Required') paper which allow producing additional copies with no extra work.

The slips are designed to be placed in light metal carriers, which fit into vertical racks in such a way that only the top part of the slip can be seen. Because of this, it is usual to reserve the top line for essential information and use the rest of the slip for less important details. It is possible to consult this whenever necessary because the slips and their carriers can easily be pushed upward in the rack.

D/Arrival	Name	Room	Type	Rate	D/Departure
How received		Who By			Date Received
Agency (if any) Account Instructions				Confirmation Date	

Whitey Slip

The set of racks holding the slips acts as a booking diary. There are normally a numbered of these racks, arranged side by side within a framework hung vertically against the wall and capable to be moved along of lifted out if necessary. Special header slips arc used to divide the content into different sections. Usually their will be a separate section for each of the next thirty days, one for each of the succeeding twelve months, then a single one for any booking beyond that. As each day is reached, the rack in question is taken out and the others moved along, so that the whole mass of information is constantly being up to date.

The slips in their carriers can be moved around just as easily within the racks. This mean that it is possible to subdivide next month's booking into weeks as soon as they start accumulate. The week themselves can be broken down to days. As we have seen, the slips can be color coded, giving a quick 'at a glance overview of the main source business.

Pink	VIP
Blue	Tour
White	Ordinary
Yellow	Travel Agent

Just as important is the fact that the slips can be kept in alphabetical order. Thus was impossible with the traditional diary, where written entries have to be made as and when the booking came in.

Density Control Chart

Larger hotels use a density chart to record their booking. With the density chart rooms are classified into groups of a similar type and no allocation of a specific room is made until the guest arrives at the hotels. This is ideal for modem hotel where all rooms are similar. With only floor levels and view from a window changing. The density chart is also more useful where the guest stay is short for entries can be quickly made and changed if necessary. As with conventional chart chance bookings, extensions, early departure, all have to be noted on a chart to make sure it is true picture of the reservation position. This is often checked by the reservation manger, who can compare the rooms let on the chart with the actual number of guests in the hotel (and due to arrive) on a given day.

Characteristic of Density Chart:

1. One chart is maintained for one month.
2. Horizontal column are date while vertical column have room number.
3. Room number is not specified, only type is specified.
4. Individual reservation is not identified with the room number until the day of arrival.
5. Booking is recorded on the chart by filling in the space using a pencil.

1. Rooms are separated according to type.
2. Overbooking is indicated by crossing the room booked.
3. Room reservation received should be looked starting from top and not from down
4. Empty space indicate room availability
5. Any cancellation and amendment is to be done from down.

Hotel having more than 150 rooms, density chart is not possible.

Density Chart is Used with A Reservation Form Advance Letting Chart

It is used for allocating rooms for specific periods and show at a glance which room are already let and how long they will be occupied. At the same time it shows which rooms are available for letting and for what periods. Many hotels use this chart in conjunction with the hotel diary, as it is not practicable to record on the chart all the details that can be entered in the diary.

It consists of vertical column, one for each day, crossed by a horizontal line for each room so that each square so formed represent one room-night. When a room is reserved the square so formed by 'room number' and the nights for which it will be occupied are crossed through in pencil, and the name of the guest is written on the line. Pencil should be used so that, in the event of cancellation or alteration of the reservation, the name and the line may be erased and replaced by another. In some hotel the line and the name are linked in after the room has been occupied, so that a permanent record is kept of when rooms were occupied and by whom.

Advance Letting Chart is Used with A Booking Diary

Diary System of Reservation

Diary system of Reservation is used by small hotel having approximately 50-60 rooms. This was one of the most common systems till Whitney system of reservation was designed and introduced. The booking diary is a useful detail recorded of the guest as it stores reservation that has been received with their date of arrival. Booking diary gives neat display and detail of guest with arrival date.

Advantages:

1. Diary is very useful for small hotel.
2. Diary system provides the records of reservation for each day in a consolidated form in a page.
3. Diary is good for those hotels where guest stay is very long.
4. Diary cannot be maintained in alphabetic order.
5. Guest status is not known at a glance.

Group Reservations

Although group reservation procedures appear simplistic, a number of potential problems may develop. The following sections consider possible solutions to some of these.

Conventions And Conferences

Problems can occur during a convention or conference if a close working relationship is not established between the hotel's sales staff and the group's meeting planner. If good communication and a spirit of cooperation are established early on, many problems can be avoided.

Housing / Convention Bureaus

Large conventions sometimes require the use of rooms at more than one hotel to accommodate all the convention attendees. Often, room requirements at several hotels are coordinated by a separate housing or convention bureau. Each hotel must determine the number and type of available rooms it is willing to set aside for convention use. The objective of the bureau is to accommodate all attendees by coordinating hotel availabilities with reservation requests. The housing/convention bureau will communicate reservation requests to the hotels involved on a daily basis. In return, each hotel informs the bureau of any requests or cancellations communicated directly to the property. Though such an exchange of information, the bureau should be able to help each hotel effectively manage its convention block.

Creating a Group Block

Group business is often highly desired by hotels. Yet, creating and controlling a group block has its pitfalls. When handling group blocks, the reservations manger should be aware of the following situations that can come into play.

- Group business demands that a contract be drawn up that specifies the exact number of rooms required and the quoted rates. The contract must also specify the group dates, and special considerations such as suites or complimentary rooms, and the group and individual billing arrangements. The contract should also note the group cut-off date for room availability.

- The reservations manager should verify the total number of rooms required for the group against what is available in the hotel. If the group will take away rooms from transient (non-group) business, the reservations manager should notify the sales or general manager of the possible effect.

- Before blocking the rooms, the reservations manager should check the group's history with the hotel - if available. For example, if the group requests a 50-room block - and the record shows the group only picked up 40 rooms the year before - the reservations manager may wish to confer with the sales manager before finalizing the block. Reducing a block based on the group's history is called a wash down or a wash. If the group dies not have a history at the hotel, it is sometimes possible to check with the hotel that last accommodated the group. By following these steps, the reservations manager helps control room inventories - and ensures that as many rooms are available for sale as possible.

Tour Groups. Tour groups are groups of people who have had their accommodations, transportation, and related travel activities arranged for them. Hotels should be especially careful to research the reliability and past performance of tour operators and travel agents. Once acquainted with a tour operator's history, reservations agents may feel more secure when blocking and booking reservations for a tour group.

Greetings & Selling

Greeting a guest is the procedure of conveying a feeling of welcome to the guest and obviously it is an activity to be carried out at the time of arrival of a guest to the hotel. Greeting procedure starts from the moment the guest drives in the portico and continues further. As his car stops it is the doorman who provides him greeting both by gestures and speaking. His gesture of saluting, smile and opening the door of the car and simultaneously wishing the guest the time of the day and further opening the door to the lobby, etc. are all together very important that both in providing welcome to the guest and greeting the guest. The bellboy or porter also is very much responsible for conveying the appropriate greeting to the guest at this time. It is important that both of these staff members (that is) the doorman and bellboy or porter realize the importance of greeting the guest. They represent the hotel, the management and other employees of the hotel. The first impression is very important and it is very true that it is the best impression as well as the lasting impression and for the guest to form a good and everlasting impression of the hotel, the management and staff it is important that he is given good welcome and greeted nicely.

The process of greeting continues further and the guest is given welcome when he reaches the front desk. The first encounter is crucial. The guest must be greeted in courteous and friendly manner.

His presence must be acknowledged as soon as he arrives at the counter. A smile of welcome from an attractive, smart, efficient and well spoken receptionist immediately creates a warm and friendly atmosphere and welcome to the guest on arrival. At times the Receptionist may be busy talking to some other person over the phone or personally, in such cases, he should excuse himself for a minute, greets the arriving guest, says "I will be with you in a minute sir", finishes his conversation with the first guest, or telephone as early as possible and attends to the waiting guest The best way to open conversation with a guest is to wish him the time of the day.

In case the guest is known greet with a pleased smile, "Good morning Mr. XYZ, nice to have you back". This creates instant link with the guest But greeting of an unknown guest is of great importance as like a known guest he will not be able to secure attention of the receptionist. The art of reception is to balance and minimize the difference in the tone of reception to two guest coming to the counter at the same time out of which one is very well known and the other is a new guest to the receptionist

The welcome procedure continues when the guest after registration is going to his room. The receptionist says to the bellboy, "James, please take Mr. XYZ to room number.

It continuous further when the guest enters the elevator and the lift attendant greets him

Assessing The Requirement of The Guest

After the guest has been received and greeted by the receptionist, the receptionist's duty is to assess his requirements (that is) whether he has a reservation or not, and further the type of room, facilities, amenities, room plans, tariff etc. he wants. At the same time to find out his choice like room facing swimming pool, near or away from the elevator or room

Importance of Product Knowledge

It is very important that the receptionist has an intimate knowledge of the product he is selling. It may appear that the product which the receptionist of a hotel has to sell is merely a bedroom or a number of bed rooms, but it is much more that in fact, and is not as simple as selling a room but far more complex. The product which he has to sell is whole range of services which the hotel has to offer to a guest depending upon its standards. This is particularly more important for a new entrant to this industry. It is suggested that he should be made to complete a checklist of the business for him, so that he is able to deal with the various possible questions which the guest may ask him from time to time during the process of selling the room to the guests.

This is further suggested that the checklist must be very detailed. Start with an analysis of location of business itself, its public areas so that he is able to show the guest the way or at least is able to direct him to what they want, its bars, restaurants, their opening and closing hours, formal or informal dress requirements etc. and other facilities and services. He should also have in his checklist the flow and lounge service details. Information about swimming pool, car hire, travels service etc. details about rooms, their rates, locations, plans.

It is generally observed that in many hotels the front office staff which is directly responsible for the sale of the room has virtually no knowledge of the rooms in terms of its location and situation, the view from its window or balcony etc. Many a times he may not have seen the room even which he is trying to sell. He may not know about the layout, its furniture, colour scheme, type and size of bed and other such facilities and amenities available in the room. Some hotel management realize this problem and allow their staff to spend a night or two in their vacant rooms to give them a fairly good idea of the product which they are required to sell later. But in busy hotels this may not be possible. Some hotels keep colour photograph of various types of rooms at the front desk. This helps the staff in equating to room requirement of the guest to the available room when shown. This would also help the potential guest in visualizing the room they are about to occupy. This is a useful aid in small hotels and where the rooms of the same type may vary in size, decoration and furnishing etc.

Some small hotels use room-cards also at the reception counter for reference of the receptionist. This card contains information about decoration and furnishing. Another use to which the room card may be put is that it would tell the receptionist effectively as to the names of the guest occupying the room in recent weeks and any complaints that have been received. In large and medium sized hotels this card is no more in use as this objective can be easily achieved by the use of visual display unit (VDU) very effectively.

Selling Techniques

The next step after having collected a detailed knowledge of the product and the requirement of the guest for a receptionist to make sure he utilizes the information for the best possible advantage and maximum sale of the product. The efforts of a receptionist would be to not only maximize the room sales and profitability of the hotel but would assist the customer in getting satisfaction. At the same time it would give a moral boost to the receptionist and an ego satisfaction that it is due to his efforts that the hotel is getting more business and the guest is satisfied. Selling more business and the guest is satisfied. Selling function in the hotel is not the same as in other industries, where evidently it appears that the salesman's function is to so - pressurize the guest by his ability to that extent that he is almost compelled to buy the product. In a hotel the selling function is purely the use of common sense to try to assist the potential or existing guest with their requirements.

Good sales is really dealing with the requirements of the customers and trying to accommodate them wherever possible in courteous manner.

In order to sell accommodation successfully the receptionist must learn how to use eyes, ears, and his intelligence in assessing of judging his potential customer. All guests differs emotionally, physically and temperamentally and will have a wide variance of their dislikes, taste etc. Many guests may require detailed guidance as to the best type of accommodation according to their needs whereas others will have fairly strong predetermined ideas of what they want. A tactful and good receptionist will be reacting accordingly.

Selling for the receptionist should become a natural part of conversation. This type of selling is more important when a walk in comes to the hotel. The prospective guest should be put at ease immediately. If the room is available the clerks ability which will help the hotel in getting the business at the terms of the hotel (that is) if the clerk is efficient and smart he may be able to sell a high priced room to the guest. Selling by the receptionist involves finding the needs of a guest, converting them into wants and providing the facilities to fulfill them. (While trying to sell room to a person who hasn't made any previous booking at the hotel, the receptionist should never quote a minimum rate rules asked for it. On the contrary he should provide the guest with a choice of rates starting from high to lower. He should try to create a mental picture of the room and its advantages and illustrate the advantages of one room over the other).

At times the receptionist may not be in a position to provide the guest a room matching his standard. In such situation a good and effective receptionist may be able to sell a lower standard room to the guest by careful reference to the facilities and cost of the room. Approach to the customer should be friendly and courteous, always and the alternative accommodation should be presented in a favorable way. The room should be described and reference made from personal knowledge of the fact that there it a television or it has been recently redecorated, there is an air-conditioner. So that the guest will become aware of.

Sales techniques must be encouraged by the Accommodation Manager as there is no doubt that if properly applied they will increase business.

Selling skills of a receptionist come to real test at the time of room assignment. He has not to merely dispense the rooms but at the same time provide the guest with the fulfillment of their needs and management satisfaction by selling the house to its advantage. The receptionist should be able to size up the guest from his questions and make offers in a way that reflects his understanding of guest requirements.

Selling face to face is a key task for, the receptionist. This means actively promoting the activities of the hotel rather than being passive, and only responding to guest enquiries and request. The receptionist must be able to develop U.S.P (Unique Sales Promotion) for the hotel that is, "This is something that occurs only in that particular unit". The product analysis will provide some useful leads which should be computed with the competitors of that area. Such examples of U.S.P's are as follows:

i. We have a covered garage.
ii. Our pool contains fresh water.
iii. We have direct dial telephones.
iv. No extra charge for children below 12 years of age.

The receptionist should have the capability of converting a negative aspect of a room situation into an advantage for the guest while explaining it to the guest. For example, a room without a good view may be called as quite room. A room near the lift may be explained as easily accessible room etc. He should use descriptive words wherever possible and some attributes of the room must be mentioned like a "Room with a view of the park".

Sandwich the price by placing it between description words and never quote the price of the room alone. For example, "A large room for Rs. 1000/- per night with a very good view from the window".

Sell high but avoid being aggressive. There is nothing worse than overdoing sales. The receptionist should try to Sell the whole hotel by making suggestion. For example, "We have a new Chinese chef who is famous for excellent food. Should I make a table reservation for you sir?", or, "The new entertainer is fantastic, the show starts at 6:30 pm in our Sapper Club, I can make a table reservation for you now sir".

Completion of Registration Card

After the guest has signed the Registration Card and has been send the room the receptionist completes the incomplete card. In a large hotel this job is done behind the reception counter that is, in the back area.

Making of The Guest Folio

Next step after the completion of Registration Card is to open a guest folio or guest bill. In some hotels this is done in the back area behind the reception counter while in some hotels the copy of completed guest registration card along with the reservation slip (if any) is sent to Bill section, who opens the guest folio or Bill for the guest.

1. Performa of guest weekly bill used in small hotels.
2. Transparency of guest folio used in NCR machine system attached.
3. In some hotels guest folio is prepared by the computer.

Arrival Notification Slip

Another job which is carried out in the back area of the reception counter of a large hotel after the guest has been registered is notification of the arrival to the concerned departments and section of the hotel.

Small hotels used a small slip called as Arrival/Departure Notification Slip for this purpose, (Performa attached).

Large hotels use Whitney Slips which are typed and circulated to all departments. Generally six copies are made and circulated to various departments as follows:

1. 2 slips to Telephone Department.
2. 1 slip to the Housekeeper.
3. 1 slip to the Room Service.
4. 2 slip to the Front desk (one to be adjusted in Numerical Rack and the second in the Alphabetical Rack).

Completion of Statutory Requirement

Preparing of "C Form" for foreigners, (everyday it is the responsibility of the Front Office staff to send the copies of the C Form to the FRRO and obtain an acknowledgement from them. The format used for that is shown in transparency.

Handling Over Booking Situation

Whenever you are over booked, this will reflect your Room position in negative, the number of rooms by which you are over booked. Therefore, overbooking situation does not come to you as a surprise, but you know it in advance that you are over booked.

Generally hotels have understanding with each other to compensate over booked guests of one another because this situation can occur in any of the Hotels. Some Hotels, as a matter of policy always keep a margin for over booking in order to compensate the shortfalls by factors like No-shows etc., due to which the occupancy pay fall. But this is only possible when you are able to sell more than your capacity- and you have that potential for selling.

The arrangements for over booked guests are made in a nearby Hotel of the same standard. Hotel also keeps the transport arrangement ready to provide complimentary transport to the over booked guests. Efforts are made to provide accommodation at the same tariff as that of your own, but in case of excess cases of over booking tactfully at arrival.

The most important decision to be taken in case of the over booking situation is that who are the guests you will shift to other hotels. The following factors are to be kept in

- Have you received advance for booking?

Keeping in mind the above, the arrangements are made for those guests with whom you will face least amount of problem at the time of arrival. However, Diplomacy and tact are required in Receptionist for handling this situation.

Reservation Cancellation

A prospective guest does the hotel a service when he or she takes the time to cancel a reservation. Reservation cancellation informs the hotel that a previously reserved room is available once again, and helps the front office update its planning. Hotels should make reservation cancellation easy and efficient. Reservation cancellation, like any guest service, requires the reservations or front office staff to be as polite, courteous, and effective as possible.

Non-Guaranteed

To cancel a non-guaranteed reservation, the reservations agent should obtain the guest's name and address, number of reserved rooms, scheduled arrival and departure dates, and reservation confirmation number, if available. This information will ensure that the correct reservation is accessed and cancelled. After recording the cancellation, the agent will assign a cancellation number and may ask the caller whether lie he or she would like to make an alternate reservation. Reservations agents must ensure that the correct reservation record is cancelled.

Credit Card Guaranteed. Most credit card companies will support no-show billings only if the hotel issues cancellation numbers for properly cancelled reservations. Reservations agents may follow a cancellation procedure for credit card guaranteed reservations which involves the following steps:

1. Obtain information from the guest to access the reservation record and verify that it is the correct one. This information includes the guest's name and address, number of rooms, scheduled arrival and departure dates, and the reservation confirmation number. After processing, the guest should be assigned a reservation cancellation number. The agent should explain that the cancellation number should be retained as. proof of cancellation in the case of an erroneous credit card billing.

2. Mark the reservation record as canceled, a properly initial and date it and add the cancellation number to the reservation record. If the cancellation is made by someone other than the guest, the reservations agent should add the caller's name to the cancelled reservation record.

3. Log the reservation cancellation number.

4. File cancelled reservation documentation for future reference, per hotel policy. Non-automated hotels commonly keep the reservation record until the expected date of arrival - just in case the reservation was cancelled by mistake. If necessary, the cancelled reservation is given to the front desk for reference and research. In automated hotels, cancelled reservations are stored electronically on computer until

Advance Deposit Policies related to the cancellation of advance deposit reservations vary greatly among hotel companies. The reservations agent should treat advance deposit cancellations with as much care as any other form of reservation cancellation. The deposit will need to be returned to the guest who property cancels a reservation. Reservations agents must exercise care when assigning and recording reservation cancellation numbers.

Other Guarante d Reservations

The person contacting the hotel to cancel a corporate account or travel agency guaranteed reservation is likely to be a representative of the corporation or travel agency - not the traveler. It is important to note the name of the person canceling the reservation on the reservation record. A reservation cancellation number should be issued and logged similar to the way a credit card guaranteed reservation number is handles. In addition, a letter documenting the cancellation may be sent to the corporate or travel agency sponsor.

Registration

Introduction

The registration process begins when the guest arrives at the reception or the arrival section of the hotel. The process terminates when he has signed the registration card or guest arrival register, has been assigned a room and goes to his room. The registration procedure differs for the different categories of the guests, like guests with reservation, without reservation, foreigners, groups, etc.

This process of registration is very important for the hotel as it not only contributes significantly to the basic information the hotel needs to monitor its business, but it is also a legal requirement. A complete record of present and past guests has to be maintained. It is a legal requirement that each guest must be registered. Guest signature is important as it signifies his consent to pay for all the services provided by the hotel and abide by the rules and regulations of the hotel. It also serves as a proof of his stay in the hotel from a certain date to another certain date. So in short, registration serves as legal contract between the hotel and the guest. We can summarize the objectives of the registration system as follows:

1. To provide guest information to he hotel.
2. To provide information about the dale of departure.

A Registration Process is Based on The Following Four Concepts.

1. Collection: It helps the hotel in capturing information pertaining to the guest needs, expected or actual date of departure, billing instructions like cash or credit, mode of payment and personal data like his occupation, date of birth, purpose of visit, his office and residential address, etc.

2. Assignment And Allocation of Room: The assignment of room matching the guest requirement both in terms of type and the rate of the room.

3. Credibility of The Guest: Based on the policies like advance payment and credit limits, etc. of the hotel and also on the basis of information provided by the billing instructions, the hotel decides upon fixing the credit limit for the guest.

4. Future Planning of The Room Sales: The hotel can maximize it's occupancy through a knowledge of room availability based on the information from the registration records.

Various Types of Registration Records

Information about the guest which may be required by the hotel or police may be registered in two ways (1) In the form of a 'Hotel Register' also known as 'Red Book'or 'F form'. (2) Individual guest 'Registration cards'.

The register can be a 'Bound Book Register' which is normally used by small hotels. Thick book which can be used for long time.

Merits:
1. All records are available in one book.
2. No filing is required.
3. Wastage is minimum.

Demerits:
1. Only one guest can register at a time.
2. It is bulky and difficult to carry to other departments.
3. Being very bulky and used for long period, it looks shabby on the counter.
4. Privacy can not be maintained.
5. Pre-registration not possible.
6. If the book is misplaced all the record is lost.

Another type of register is a 'Loose Leaf Register' which is same as the bound book register in it's contents but the pages are not bound. One page or sheet is used for each day.

1. To some extent privacy is ma itained.
2. Easy to hand over to customer to write details.
3. If one sheet is lost only one day's record is lost.
4. If for a day, one full sheet is not completed, the rest goes waste.
5. Only one guest can register at a time.
6. Filing becomes an additional job.

Individual guest registration cards are most widely used in hotels these days. They may be duplicate or triplicate depending on the hotel.

Merits:
1. Many guests may be registered at the same time.
2. Privacy can be maintained.
3. Storage is easy.
4. No wastage.
5. Guests can be pre registered.
6. More mobile.

Demerits:
1. Expensive.
2. If not properly stored, may be lost.

Documents Generated in The Registration Process
1. **Registration Card:** Used to collect guest personal data.
2. **Room Rack Slip:** A document on which the information is transferred from the registration card in the form of a summary. This slip is placed in the room rack.

3. **Information Rack Slip:** Used to provide guest name and room no. A copy of this slip goes to room service, housekeeping, telephones, etc. These departments also maintain information racks.

4. **Bell Boy's Errand Card:** It is communicate the guest arrival to the bell desk and to keep a check on the movement of the bell boys.

Other Support Documents

i. **Arrival Notification Slips:** These slips are prepared and distributed to all (he concerned departments.

ii. **'C' Form:** The Registration of Foreigners Act 11939 Section 3(c) Rule 14 makes it obligatory on the part of the hotel to send information about the foreigners registered at the hotel. In this connection any person who is not an Indian National or one who does not hold an Indian passport is termed as a foreigner. The form which is used to notify F.R.K.O. (Mumbai, Calcutta, Chennai, Madras) is called as 'C' form. Within 24 hours from the lime of registration of a foreigner (12 hours for Pakistani, Chinese and other middle eastern countries) the information should reach the F.R.R.O. In the cities where there arc no F.R.K.O. this information should reach the office of the Superintendent of Police of that area or town. Nepal and Bhutan and Shree Lanka nationals are exempted from the 'C' form notification. The 'C' form is made in duplicate pr in triplicate. It is made in duplicate if sent to F.R.R.O. (original copy goes to F.R.R.O.). If it is sent to the S.P. office, it has to be made in triplicate (two copies sent to the S.P. office). A bell boy is debuted to do this work everyday and it is his duty to bring the acknowledgment of their receipt from the F.R.R.O. The 'C' forms arc serially numbered and contain all the information about he guest which is collected from the G.R. card (guest registration card).

Registration System Problems

Various problems which may make the Reservation system ineffective are as follows :

- Inaccurate room availability information resulting in improper room assignment.
- Inadequate and incomplete information about guest, his expected date of departure etc.
- Improper co-ordination with Housekeeping regarding room status reporting.
- Lack of efficiency in making of supporting documents like room Rack slip and Information slip etc.

Types of Registration Systems

Non-Automatic Systems: it refers to a manual system. This system is used for small hotels where the installation of automatic system would prove to be quite expensive and waste. All the forms like 'C' form, room rack slip, information rack slip, arrival notification slip, etc. are produced and distributed manually. It is wholly dependent on guests accurate and legible completion of the registration card.

1. **Semi-Automatic System:** It is a combination of manual and automated systems which involves the usage of the office machinery, clerical equipment and people.

2. **Fully Computerised System:** It is system in which various section of the front office department are connected to each other with the help of computer interfaces. The data collected at one point can be transmitted and utilized at any other location, this system speeds up the Process And Reduces The No.of Errors.

Room Selling Techniques Upselling Rooms

Mark Gordon an experienced F. O. & GM trains his staff in 3 non pressure selling techniques. They are especially effective in inducing guests to accept medium-priced and deluxe rooms instead of minimum - rate accommodations this techniques are.

1. The Choice - of - Door Technique

The FOA gives the guest a choice of rate categories and asks, "which would you prefer"? No presume is applk d, the guest does that all by himself. People tend to avoid extremes and are likely to select the middle choice. Thus a guest being offered a room are of Rs. 4000. Rs. 5000 or Rs. 6000 will likely go for the Rs.5000 room even if he had planned on the lowest rate.

2. The Door-in-The-Face Technique

This approach has to be handled with fact and without presume. It can result in drastic increase of the average rate per occupied room. FOAs start from the top down quoting the highest priced room in the category the guest wishes.

A single room on our club floor, with patio and sitting room at Rs.7,500/-. The guest may accept this or ask for something less expensive, at which the FOA quotes the next date down, say the Deluxe room on the 4th floor with KB and view of the garden at Rs.6800". By comparison this room still appears of above average quality but considerably less expensive than the previously quoted one. According to the theory of reciprocity, many guests will be convinced that after rejecting the highest rate, accepting the middle rate room is a rational compromise.

3. The Foot-in-The-Door Technique

This technique is based on the notion that people who have already agreed to one proposition will quite easily agree to another one. The reservationist while taking a reservation over the phone or selling a room over the counter can use this by saying, 'We arc holding a std. room in the East wing for you, Mr. Sharma for an extra Rs.500 you have a deluxe room in our lake view wing or for Rs. 600 per person you can take advantage of our week end package, which includes the American b'fast in your room plus dinner for two at the Zodiac grill. The guest can simply say "no, thank you" or accept the upsale suggestion.

Upselling is not a game or a way to squeeze extra rupees out of unsuspecting travellers. It should be part of a professional receptionists and guest services representatives repertoire. It should be seen as one more way to

i. Provide better services to the guests by offering choices.

ii. Increase rooms revenue for the hotel.

Upselling Techniques

1. Know the product

2. Control the encounter

Ask specific questions such as, "we have a quiet double room on our. Silver floor. Is that suitable for you?" Avoid asking open-ended questions, such as 'what kind of

3. Sell high, but avoid high-pressure selling techniques

4. Turn a negative aspect of a room or rooming situation into an advantage for the guest eg. A room without a view becomes a quiet room. A room near the elevator or near the busy pool may be noisy but is 'handy' and easily accessible if you plan

5. Sandwich the price between descriptive phrases, "one of our extra - large rooms at Rs. 6,500/- plus tax overlooking the garden" or quote the price of more than one

   "We have double rooms for Rs. 6500/- but the ones with the new mini bar are Rs. 6,800/- "

6. Ask for the sale

   Once all the information has been presented to the guest the FOA must gently but resolutely, close the sale. "If that is a suitable choice, may I ask you to sign the registration card', is an effective way to move negotiations to a close.

7. Listen to guest conversational comments, such as "Oh what a hot day 11 could do with something cool". They will help to determine their needs better and to sell other services of the hotel. "Our outdoor pool and bar are still open."

8. Sell the whole hotel by making suggestions for dinner. "Just dial 7 on your room phone to make a reservation" or for drinks in the lounge "The new entertainer is fantastic' and for recreational facilities. "There is no charge for the use of the Sauna and the health club".

9. Try to anticipate the guest's needs and offer services, suggestions, and assistance.

Report Generated:
- ✓ In house guest list (alphabetical list)
- ✓ In house guest list (Room numberwise)
- ✓ Departure Reports

Individual Guest Registration Card (GRC)

Individual Registration Cards are used by various hotels these days. They may be used in duplicate or triplicate depending from hotel to Hotel. These are given to guest at the time of arrival for completion of registration.

Following Are its Merits And Demerits :

Merits:
- Many guests may be registered at the same time
- Privacy can be maintained
- If not properly stored they may be lost.

Registration System Problems

Various problems which may make the Reservation system ineffective are as follows:
- Inaccurate room availability information resulting in improper room assignment

- Inadequate and incomplete information about guest his expected date of departure etc.
- Improper co-ordination with Housekeeping regarding room status reporting.
- Lack of efficiency in making of supporting documents like room Rack slip, and Information slip etc.

Non-Automated System

The non-automatic system refers to manual system. This system is used for a small hotel where the installation of automatic system would prove to be quite expensive and waste. A small hotel will obviously have a low volume of business. In a manual system all documents are produced by people. In a non-automatic system at the time of arrival the guest is provided with a registration card or an arrival register. In a medium sized hotel the registration card is given to the guest in a folder or on a registration card holder with a pen. Registration card holder is a piece of front office equipment used by guest. The guest fills up this card and puts his signature. The subsequent documents like arrival notification slip (Rack slips), 'C' form (in case of foreigner) or any other are prepared by transferring the relevant information from the card. The documents are produced and distributed manually. Similarly a pre-registration is followed. There is no need of any sophisticated equipment but waste of resources. This system as already said is good for a small or medium sized hotel. A non-automatic system for registration is wholly dependent on guests* accurate and legible compilation of a Registration card.

Semi Automated System

A semi automatic system is a combination of system which involves the usage of office machinery, clerical equipment, and people. In this system of registration the collection of data and information from the guest at the time of his arrival is done the same way as in the case of manual system (i.e.) on a Registration card, but the use of office equipment typewriter for example is done to type out the rack slips neatly and also to type the top/heading information on guest folios. Further the slips are transmitted to various departments like Room service, Housekeeping and telephones either manually or sometime mechanically through the usage of pneumatic tubes.

Fully Automated System

A fully automatic registration system is composed of computer equipment and electronic devices at the reception section of the front desk. In this system the reservation process and registration process are linked together and the registration system is an integral part of reservation system. From the reservation records the file data is transferred to registration programme. The interfacing of Reservation and Registration enables the system to print out a registration card with the use of printer in the form of hard copy as well as a screen display, a soft copy. This system provides a very smooth, accurate and speedy guest check-in. This can perform pre-registration activities also. A small business card size identification card for the guest may also be produced. All other documents necessary can, also be produced subsequently from data stored in computer's brain memory. The pre-registration guest room assignment and on-line-status Inquiry facilities aster check-in, giving the staff more time to care on guest services, for a walk-in the front desk clerk may just use a normal registration card to collect the information from the guest who has come for the first time and later enter the information into the system via a terminal with the help of a key board or may directly transfer the information into VDI(Visual Display Interface) as he collects it from the guest verbally for computer to process the registration information. The computer programme requires that a set of specific information should be provided in a set manner for processing.

By the use of computer system, where registration information are entered into computer memory various automatic reports (which normally take a long time to prepare) like expected departures list, In-house guest lists, group rooming list, forecasted revenue generation etc. can be obtained very easily in no time and most accurately.

Registration Handling Functions - Some of The Main Features:

- Pre-registers reserved guests / groups by assigning rooms prior to their arrival- Today's arrival.
- Print Registration cards with guest's details already filled in.
- Check-in guests with reservations.
- Check-in- walk in guests.
- Display the status of rooms by specifying the status for which inquiry is to be made.
- Modify in-house guest information.
- Inquire about in-house guest information
- Inquire about in-house guest information.
- Inquire about in-house guests by giving name / room number / group ID / guest class / company ID / Room type / Rate code etc.
- More guest to a new room. The bills belonging to the guest will automatically get transferred to the new room.

Reports Generated

- ✓ In house guest list (alphabetical list).
- ✓ In-house guest list (Room number-wise).
- ✓ Departure Reports (Numerical according to Room wise).
- ✓ In-house complimentary and staff occupied rooms report.

When Guests Can Not Be Accommodated

In general, a hotel is obligated to accommodate guests. Discrimination is prohibited in places of public accommodation on the basis of race, sex, religion, or national origin. Legitimate reasons for refusing to accommodate a guest may include a lack of available rooms, or the potential guest's drunk or disorderly behavior or unwillingness to pay for hotel services. State laws may stipulate other reasons for denial, a front desk agent should never be the person who determines whether someone will be roomed or not. This is the responsibility of management. Management is also responsible for informing the person that he or she has been turned away. Management, with the advice of legal counsel and the state hotel association, should instruct the front office staff on policies and procedures concerning the acceptance or rejection of potential guests.

On occasion, a hotel may be short of available rooms and may not be able to accommodate guests. It is imperative that the hotel set policies for handling these situations. Seldom, if ever should a hotel be unable to accommodate a guest with a reservation - especially a guaranteed reservation. When this happens, most hotels will make other arrangements for the guest. In the case of a guaranteed reservation, most luxury hotels will pay for the guest's room at another property. It is important to remember that the hotel may have no obligation to guests without guaranteed reservations, or to guests who arrive after the cancellation hour (often 6:00 p.m.). Generally speaking, guests with reservations who arrive before the cancellation hour should be accommodated.

Walk-in-Guests

The classic nightmare for the tired walk-in guest is to travel for miles and miles only to find that the hotel is booked. If a walk-in guest cannot be accommodated, front desk agents can make the situation a little easier for the guest by suggesting and providing directions to alternative hotels nearby.

Most of the time, guests who cannot be accommodated at the hotel would prefer to say at a similar property. Hotel should keep a list, with phone numbers, of comparable properties in the local area. Hotels can reap some significant benefits through mutual guest referrals. For one, guest referrals allow one hotel to compare how well it is doing on a given night with other area hotels. Competent properties, too, may reciprocate by sending their overflow business to the hotel. But mainly, referrals should be viewed as a guest relations tool. The extra care paid to walk-in guests helps create an industry-wide atmosphere of

The situation may be more difficult when a walk-in guest believes he or she has a reservation. A hotel might take the following steps to clarify the situation:

- ❖ If the guest presents a letter of confirmation, verify the date and the name of the hotel; the guest may have arrived on a different date or at the wrong property. Most confirmation letters have a confirmation number which will help the front desk agent locate the reservation. Ask whether another person made the reservation for the guest; the reservation may be at another property, or it may be misfiled under the

- ❖ Double-check the reservation file in view of the guest; perhaps the reservation was for another date.

- ❖ Double-check the reservations file for another spelling of the last name. For instance, B, P, and T are often confused in a telephone conversation. Also check to see if the first and last names were reversed in the reservation file.

- ❖ If the reservation made through a travel agency or representative, allow the guest to call that source for clarification.

- ❖ Ask the guest to confirm his or her arrival data, the guest may be arriving on a different day or a day late. Many hotels hold no-show registration cards from the previous day in the front of the registration file Justin case a no-show comes in a day late.

If there seems to be no alternative to waking - turning away - the guest, a manager - not a front desk agent - should explain the matter in a private office. Registering one guest in view of another who cannot be accommodated can be extremely awkward.

Guests with Non-Guaranteed Reservations

A number of situations or circumstances can delay a guest's scheduled arrival. Guests frequently do not have the chance to change a non-guaranteed reservation to a guaranteed reservation by the time they realize they will arrive post the hotel's reservation cancellation hour. As a result, the hotel may not hold the room for the guest and may not have a room available when arrives. If the hotel cannot provide a guest room, front desk agents must be extremely tactful hen informing the guest. Blame should not be placed on anyone's shoulders since the lack of accommodations is neither the guest's nor the hotel's fault.

Guests with Guaranteed Reservations

If reservations are carefully handled and good forecasting procedures are followed, the property should never have to deny accommodations to a guest with a guaranteed reservation. Nonetheless, a property should have a policy for front desk staff to follow in such situations.

A manager should take charge and make necessary decisions when it appears the property will not have accommodations for a guest with a guaranteed reservation. This

- ✓ Review all front desk transactions.

- ✓ Take an accurate count of rooms available, using all relevant data.

- ✓ Compare the room rack, housekeeper's report, and guest folios for discrepancies.

- ✓ Telephone due-outs - guests expected to check out today - who have not checked out and confirm their check-out time. If they do not answer the telephone, physically check the guest rooms to verify occupancy. The guest may have left the hotel without stopping at the front desk. The guest may also have expected to be billed, or may have paid in advance, and forgot to check out at the front desk. Finally, an early discovery of a skipper - that is, a guest who leaves with no intention of paying for the room — will allow the guest room to be rented by another guest.

- ✓ Personally check all out-of-order rooms. Could an out-of-order room be readied for sale if necessary? If a guest would be willing to occupy and out-of-order room as is, should the room be rented or its rate adjusted? These decisions must be made by management and used to the hotel's written policies.

All Front Desk Staff Should Be Consistent When Discussing The Lack of Accommodations With Arriving Guests. Some Helpful Suggestions Include:

- ✓ Guests may be encouraged to return to the hotel at the earliest date of availability. Upon their return, they may be placed on a VIP list and presented with a small gift as compensation for the inconvenience of being turned away.

- ✓ A follow-up letter may be sent to guest who arrived with a reservation but could not be accommodated, apologizing again for the inconvenience and encouraging the guest to consider returning to the hotel at some future time.

- ❖ If a member of a convention block cannot be accommodated, the group's meeting planner should be notified. The planner may be able to solve the problem by arranging for some attendees to double up. In such situations, it is important for the front office to have a good working relationship with the meeting planner.

- ❖ If a member of a tour group cannot be accommodated, the tour organizer should be notified immediately and the situation explained. This notification may better enable the organizer to deal with any membership complaints in a timely fashion.

- ❖ The hotel may pay the transportation expenses associated with having the guest travel to an alternative property. Financial considerations are especially important when walking a guest with a guaranteed reservation.

Visa Rules And Regulations

The basic rules on grant of visa/extension of stay to foreigners have been laid down in Visa Manual (updated upto March 1989). Several amendments/relaxation have been made since then. A number of modifications, additions and deletions have taken place in respect of these instructions since then and MHA have issued circulars to the concerned authorities form timeto time. A gist of the circulars / instructions issued by MHA/MEA is given in the succeeding paragraphs.

Types of Visa

A. Conference Visa Without Prior Reference By Govt

Indian Missions and Posts abroad have been given powers to issue visa to the bonafide foreign participants to conferences which are held by the government bodies, public sector undertaking to aided bodies, without prior reference to the Government of India, provided their names do not appear on the Suspect Index and the Missions are satisfied about the bonafide purpose of the visit. (MHA No.)

B. Employment Visa

A separate category of visa for employment purposes, namely 'E' Visa (denoting employment) has been introduced since August 1994. Indian Missions and Posts abroad have been authorized to grant 'E' Visa to foreigners initially for a period of one year. It should be restricted only to skilled and qualified personnel, who are appointed by companies, organizations, and Industrial / Economic undertakings etc. on contract or employment in senior levels and in possession of valid documents to prove the same. Family members of such foreigners who arc granted 'E' type of visa may be granted 'X' visas and its validity should be co-terminus with the validity of visas of their spouses or for such shorter period, as considered necessary. Foreign technicians/experts coming to Indian in pursuance of bilateral agreements may be granted Employment Visa up to a period of S years subject to instructions issued earlier vide MHA circular letter no. (250022/13/90-FI, dated 21.6.90).

C. Journalists Are Issued 'J' Visas Only

It is mandatory for all Missions to issue T Visas for journalists applying for visa t visit India, irrespective of the purpose for which they are making the visit. Even if the request for visa is for a period of less than three months, the standard period for grant of visa should be three months. (MEA Letter No VII/406/I6/94, dated 4.8.94).

D. Student Visa Foreigners Holding Student Visa And Doing Phd/Research in India

It has been decided that foreign scholars who having arrived on student visa are now pursuing Research studies may approach the nodal Ministry concerned or Ministry of Human Research

Development for conversion of their visa into research visas from student visa before 31.5.98. Prior security clearance of MHA in all such cases will be necessary.

- ❖ ICCR will also act as the nodal agency in respect of foreign Scholar coining under Cultural Exchange Programme.
- ❖ M.Phil., Ph.D. Casual Research, Research which is part of the Ph.D. would all come within the ambit of Research Visa.

(Ref: MHA No 25022/24/98-F.I, dated 29.4.98)

E. Tourist Visa

It has been decided that three months Tourist Visa should be done away with and henceforth only six months Tourist Visa may be granted to foreigners. The six months Tourist Visa shall invariably be multiple - entry, shall be non-extendable, non-convertible and shall come into effect from date of issue. Pee to be charged for six months Tourist Visa shall be US $30.

The above decision shall not apply to specific categories like nationals of Pakistan, Bangladesh, Afghanistan, Sri Lanka, Iran, Somalia etc.

(MHA Circular No 25022/144/97-FI, Dt. 13.6.97 and 25022/144/97-FI, Dt. 30.7.97)

F. Tourist Visa Not Convertible To Other Types of Visa

Foreigners coming on Tourist Visa are not eligible to convert the tourist Visa into any kind of visa. However, this is not applicable to foreigners of Indian origin. The foreigners of Indian Origin can get extension of stay of 5 yean with multi entry facility even if they have entered on a tourist visa.

(MHA No. 25022/183/90-FI Dt. 6.6.91)

G. Special Tourist Visas For 30 Days

A special tourist visa for 30 days has been introduced on the insistence of Ministry of Tourism. The validity of these special tourist visas will be counted from the date of the first entry into India and not from the date of issue. However, first entry should be made within a period of 30 days form the date of issue.

(MHA NO. 25022/140/85 F.l Dt. 5.8.92)

H. Long Term Tourist Visa To Tour Operators Etc.

The duration of tourist visa has been raised form 4 months to six months with multi-entry facility. Travel agent's of foreign travel agencies and also granted multi entry visa for a period of 5 years by Indian Missions provided the missions are satisfied about the bona-fide purpose of the foreigners. However, stay in India on any particular visit may not exceed six months and hence thy will not be subject to registration unless their stay exceeds six months.

(MHANo. 25022/13/90-F.I, dt. 10.10.90)

Indian Missions abroad have been authorized to grant long term Tourist visas for five years, only to foreigner who is connected with tourism trade, or is frequent visitor and who will not indulge in activities other than tourism with the stipulation that the period of stay during each period shall not exceed six months.

(MHA Circular no. 25022/85/97-F.I, dated 9.9.97)

I. Grant of Visitors Visa

All foreign nationals of Indian origin who want to make short term visit to India to meet their relatives and families or for other such purposes etc. may be granted only short-term 'Visitors Visa' of category 'X' for the Relevant duration. This is to distinguish between those coming for Tourism and going to various places for some purposes and those coming for other non-tourism purposes for limited duration.

(MHA NO. 25022/50/89, dated 3.4.89)

J. Long Term Visa To U.S Citizens on Reciprocal Basis

Business and Tourist Visas wi:h 10 years validity has been introduced for the U.S nationals on reciprocal basis, with the stipulation the period of stay shall not exceed.

(MHA CIRCULAR NO. 25022/89/97-F2, DATED 20.1.98)

K. Long Term Visa- Categories of Foreigners Categories Foreigner Allowed 5 Years Multi-Entry Visa

The Indian Missions/Posts have been empowered to grant 5 years multi entry visa to the following foreign national:

Foreign technicians/experts coming to India in pursuance of bilateral agreement between the Govt, of India and the Foreign Govt, or in bilateral agreement between the foreign and Indian firm provided the agreement has been approved by the Govt, of India - Missions may grant necessary visa for the duration of the agreement or for a period of 5 years whichever is less with multiple entry facilities provided they are satisfied that the foreigner is coming t India in pursuance of bilateral agreement which has been approved by the Govt, of Indian subject to usual checks.

Foreign businessmen who want to come to India to establish industrial / business ventures or to explore possibilities to set up industrial/business ventures- Missions may grant multi-entry visa for a period of 5 years provided they are satisfied about the bonafide purpose of the foreigner and also subject to usual security checks.

Foreign students coming to India to pursue regular academic studies in India- Missions may grant visas for the duration of the course or for a period of 5 years whichever is less.

Foreign students coming to India for studying Yoga, Vedic Culture etc. and foreign students coming to India for studying Indian Systems of dancing, music, etc. - Missions may grant visas for the duration of the course or for a maximum period of 5 years whichever is less to bonafide foreign students coming to India to join well known institutions without prior reference to the Ministry.

Travel agents of foreign travel agencies and also foreign tourists visiting India frequently - Missions may grant multi-entry visa for a period of five years, at their discretion subject to the usual checks and provided they are satisfied abut the bonafied purpose to the foreigner. However, stay in India on any particular visit may not exceed six months.

First degree relatives and family members of foreigners including diplomatic personnel staying in India on Long Term basis - Mission may grunt visa for the required period or for a maximum period of five years, at their discretion, subject

(Mha No. 25022/13/90 -Fi, Dated 21.6.90)

L. Transit Visa/ Landing Permits Temporary Landing Permit

Temporary landing permit is given to foreign nationals transiting through India without valid visa provided he has a confirmed onward journey ticket. Temporary landing facility upto a period of 15 days is granted to foreign nationals coming to India without valid visa in an emergency situation like death / serious illness in the family or any technical lapse in visa etc. subject to the satisfaction of the immigration officers. However, the facility shall not be granted to nationals of Sri Lanka, Bangladesh, Pakistan, Iran Afghanistan, Somalia, Nigeria, Ethiopia and Algeria.

If the above foreign nationals do land in India without visa they should not be allowed to leave the airport/port/post and they should be put on the first available flight/vessel for their destinations. In respect of other foreign nationals coming to India without visa, immigration officers will have discretion to grant landing permit for a period of 72 hours or till the departure of the confirmed onward journey/flight. The immigration officers will retain passport of such foreign nationals and they will be issued a receipt to facilitate their movement out of the airport/port/post.

Foreign tourists in groups of four or more arriving by air or sea, sponsored by recognized Indian travel agencies may be granted collective landing permit for a period upto 30 days on the written request of the travel agencies to immigration officers;

(MHA NO. 25022/121/91 FI, DATED 2.7.91)

M. Grant of Landing Permit Facility To Minor Children

Minor children of foreign nationality whether of Indian origin of otherwise coming to India independently or accompanied by parents may be granted landing permit upto 90 days. Such children are exempted from the requirement of registration but are required to seek extensions if they want to extend their stay, which may be granted to them on application.

(MHA NO 25022/39/94 FI)

N. Transit Visa Valid For Direct Transit Only

A transit visa is valid for direct transit only irrespective of the period of stay in transit, which is not more than 15 days. This period is not ordinarily extended. For a stay I India beyond 15 days appropriate visa is to be obtained.

(MHA NO. 25022/183/90 - FI, DATED 28.1.91)

O. Landing Permit Persons In Direct Transit

Persons in direct transit, in case they desire to resume their journey by the next regularly scheduled flight, they will be allowed to land on a landing permit the validity of which will not normally exceed 15 days.

(MHA NO. 25011/183/90 - F.I, DATED 28.1.91)

Introduction of Visa Stickers

It has been decided to permit the use of visa stickers for visas to be issued form 1.8.98. Stickers would be made obligatory for all visas issued form 1st October 1998 and rubber stamp visas issued or after 1.10.98 would not be recognized at any of the entry points in India. Entries on the Visa Sticker would normally be made by hand.

(Ref. MEA NO VII/401/1/97, DATED 26.6.98)

Introduction of Visa Sticker: Clarification By Mea

All immigration checkpoints in India have been advised not to turn back passengers arriving with Rubber Stamp Visa issued by any Indian Mission/Posts even after 1.10.98. Instead, holders of such visas should be allowed entry (provided the Immigration Officer is satisfied that the Rubber Stamp Visa is not a forged one) and the details of such visas issued should be immediately communicated to the CPV Division of the MEA.

(Ref. MEA NO VIII/401/1/97, DATED 28.9.98)

Visa Fee/Visa Feb Free/Visa Free

1. Visa Fees

It has been decided to fix visa fee for all categories at the following rate w.e.f 01.01.95

i. Transit Visa (Single/Double entry): US $ 5

ii. Visa valid upto three months (multiple entry): US $ 20

iii. Visa valid upto six months (multiple entry): US $ 40

iv. Visa valid upto one year (multiple entry)

v. Student Visa (multiple entry)

vi. All visas with validity between one to five years

US$50 US$50 US $ 100

(Multiple Entry)

(MEA CIRCULAR NO VII/406/16/94, DATED 4.10.94)

2. Visa Fee Free Regime

Visa Fee Free regime exists with the following countries:

i. Afghanistan

ii. Bangladesh

iii. Greece (Deleted vide MHA no. 25022/356/97-FI, dated 10.9.98)

iv. Sweden

v. South Africa

vi. Poland

(MEA CIRCULAR NO. 25022/356/97 - FI DATED 6.1.98) @ MHA vide their no. 25022/356/97 - FI dated 10.9.98 has informed that the name of Greece was inadvertently put in the list of countries under "Visa Fee Free Regime". Hence, the name of Greece may be deleted from the list.

3. Visa Free Regime
A visa free regime to all Indian check-posts exists with:

- Bhutan and Nepal - for all passport holders
- Denmark, Belarus, Singapore, and Hongkong for all diplomatic and official passport holders.
- Germany, for diplomatic passport holders for stay upto 90 days
- Vietnam, Argentina, Ecuador, Paraguay, Maldives, Mauritius for diplomatic and official passport holders for stay upto 90 days.

Foreign nationals holding passports issued by or on behalf of the government of Maldives may be exempted from the requirement of visa provided their stay does not exceed 90 days in India. The period of 90 days shall include any prior period of such foreigner in India during a period of six months immediately before the date of his entry into India.

(MEA ID NOTES NO. VII/407/13/98, DATED 29.1.98)

(MEA UO No. 25022/2/90 - F.I DATED 1.3.90)

The government of India has decided to waive the visa requirements for diplomatic and official passport holders of the Slovak Republic, coming to India for official purposes w.f. January 10, 1995 subject to conditions that:

i. An advance notice of 15 days will be given to competent authorities in India
ii. Entry into India will be through an international airport in India
iii. Length of stay in India will rot exceed 90 days.

(MEA LETTER NO. VII/406/9/94, DATED 6.1.95)

4. Saarc Visa Exemption Scheme
Following categories of persons have been included in the SAARC Visa Exemption Scheme:

i. Supreme Court Judges
ii. Members of National Parliament
iii. Heads of National Academic Institutions
iv. Foreign/ permanent Secretaries dealing with Foreign Affairs.
v. Directors of the SAARC Secretariat.
vi. Presidents of National Chambers of Commerce and Industry.
vii. Accompanying spouse(s) and dependent children below the age of 18 years of the

(MEA UO No 25022/114A/95-FI, dated 26.07.97)

Countries Under Prior Reference Category (Prc)

All Somalian Nationals On Prior Approval Categories.

In view of the sudden increase in the number of Somalis seeking admission in Indian Educational Institutions, etc, and in order to regulate the inflow of Somalis it has been decided to put Somalian nationals on prior approval category.

(CCB No 5163, dated 26.6.91)

Bell Desk Activities

Baggage Handling on Arrival For:

F.I.T.'s

1. On arrival at the hotel porch, the doorman opens the car door for the guest to alight. Greets and welcomes him to the hotel.

2. He enquires from the guest the number of piece of baggage and takes them out placing the baggage at the baggage arrival area. He re-confirms with the guest the number of pieces of baggage.

3. The doorman then calls the porter who picks up the baggage and escorts the guest to the reception. Leaving the baggage at the bell desk.

4. While the guest is going through check-in formalities, the porter fills up the arrival errand card and tags the baggage. He presents the errand card to the receptionist who writes down the room number and passes on the keys to the porter. The porter notes the room and guests name on the baggage tags and waits for the guest to be

5. At this stage the porter should politely bring to the notice of the guest any damage that may have been caused to the baggage in the journey.

6. After the receptionist has announced the room to the guest the porter requests the guest to follow him and leads the guest to the elevator.

7. When the elevator arrives he steps aside and allows the guest to enter the lift first. He brings in the baggage and position himself near the control panel, selects the right floor and on arrival at the floor again allows the guest to leave the elevator first, giving brief directions about the location of his room for e.g. your room is straight down the corridor to the left sir.

8. He then once again leads the guest towards his room. On reaching the room the porter gently raps on the door or presses the door-bell and waits for a short while. He now inserts the room key in the lock and gently opens the door. He takes a quick peep to see if all is right in the room. He switches on the light and allows the guest to enter the room, following with the baggage himself. He places the baggage on the baggage rack and that which requires to be hanged for e.g. overcoats etc. he hangs on hangers in the closet. Vanity box being placed on the sink shelf in the bathroom.

9. He then proceeds to draw the curtains and explains the following hotel and room services - Music console, fresh potable water supply, hot water supply, TV and its operation and the programme schedule, Air-conditioning control (Checking with the guest whether the temperature is ok) main light switch, fire escape plan, house telephone guide, refrigeration, room service, guest stationery, laundry list, sewing kit and their location in the room etc.

10. While he is introducing the guest to the services above he makes a mental note of any deficiencies in the room/bathroom.

11. He now leaves the guest room wishing the guest a pleasant stay. He refrains from soliciting tips but if offered by the guest he accepts it graciously and thanks him.

12. On his way back to the lobby he gets in touch with the floor housekeeper and tells her of any deficiencies that he noted in the room.

13. On reporting to the bell desk he hands over the arrival errand card to the bell caption who makes entries in the lobby attendant control sheet.

Handling Vip Baggage

VIP baggage is to be handled in a fashion similar to the FIT baggage expect that since VIPs generally are escorted to their rooms either by the PRO or lobby Manager the porter collects the room keys and proceeds to the room with the guest baggage in advance of the

He switches on the lights, draw the curtain checks the room for any deficiencies and gets them rectified. He waits outside the room for guests to arrive. On arrival of the guest he

Group Baggage Handling

1. From the group movement sheet the bell caption confirms group arrival schedules and arranges staff accordingly to man the shifts.

2. He deputes the porters to off load the cars/coaches and before the offloaded cars/coaches leave the hotel porch last checks are made to ensure no guest belongings have been left behind

3. The baggage is collected at the bell desk ensuring that no other baggage mixes with the group baggage.

4. The bell captain counts the number of pieces and informs the tour leader. If any damage is noticed on any baggage this is brought to the notice of the T/L.

5. The bell captain confirms the rooming with the reception and the baggage is tagged. (Normally group baggage for convenience always has the travel agents name tags on them). With the help of the rooming list the baggage of each room is identified.

6. The group baggage is now sorted out room wise and wing wise.

7. Using baggage trolleys the baggage is taken to the floors. On the floors the porter noiselessly and quickly delivers the baggage to the rooms checking with the guest whether all his baggage has reached or not. The porter then explains the room facilities to the guest and before leaving wish the guest a comfortable and pleasant stay.

10. In the meanwhile the bell captain in the lobby supervises the dispatch of the baggage to the floors and checks with the tour-leader for baggage down date and timings.

Notes

1. It is important to bear in mind that a guest is most pleased if his baggage is delivered to his room in time. A guest on a visit to any country and city attaches a great deal of importance to baggage. One cannot expect the guest to settle down until his baggage has been delivered.

2. While carrying baggage on a trolley the heaviest baggage should be at the bottom. Also the baggage should be carried with their top side or the side that opens facing inwards towards the leg of the porter.

3. The wheels of the trolley should be well oiled and greased so that the squeaky and irritating sound of the wheels does not distract the guests. However avoid excessive oiling for oil drops can cause stains on carpets and floors which may be very

Baggage Handling During Departure

A guest wishing to check-out normally calls the bell desk or reception. Irrespective of where the call is received the following procedure is adopted at departure.

1. The bell captain deploys a page-cum-porter who in turn fills up the departure

2. He on this way to the guest room informs the reception and cash section about the

3. On arrival at the room he either knocks gently or presses the door bell and then himself.

4. He greets the guest and checks with him the number of pieces of baggage that are to be taken to the lobby.

5. He picks up the baggage and places it outside the room and returns to collect the key.

6. He takes a quick look around the room to check for any perceptible damages to hotel property or losses and mentally ticks off the availability of blankets, pillows, towels, vacuum flask etc.

7. He also checks for any left behinds in drawers, closets etc and having carried out the check proceeds to draw the curtains and switches off the light He then leaves the room after locking it.

8. At the elevator he allows the guest to step in first and then positions himself near the control panel with the baggage in a comer next to him.

9. He enquires of the guest politely whether he enjoyed his stay and whether he would like a taxi called for him.

10. He escorts the guest to the cash counter and he proceeds to the bell desk with the baggage.

11. He pastes hotel stickers on the baggage and marks 'D' on the hotel name tags.

12. He then comes to the cash counter and picks up the baggage out pass from the cashier.

13. He hands over the key to the reception and takes an acknowledgement from the reception.

14. He then asks the commissionaire to call a taxi and after the showing the baggage out pass to the commissionaire places the baggage in the boot of the taxi. He notes the taxi number on the errand card and also the time.

15. He then informs the guest his baggage has been placed in the boot of the taxi indicates towards the open boot for the guest to check and then closes the boot.

16. He then returns to the bell desk to complete the errand card and shows it to bell captain who signs it and makes an entry in the lobby attendant control sheet.

A group departure by and large is handled by all concerned sections of the front office in a fashion similar to FIT departure, except that a team of page boys are engaged simultaneously in clearing guest baggage. The stress is on co-ordination and efficiency and therefore a group departure demands careful supervision. Elicited below are the slightly different and some special procedural steps that are to be borne in mind. These may be in addition to the regular procedure shown n the proceeding pages.

1. The bell captain ensures sufficient staff is available in the shift.
2. He checks the group wake call and baggage down timings.
3. Five minutes before baggage down timings the bell captain allocates the floors and
4. rooms to the porters for bringing baggage down.
5. The porters collect the baggage from rooms mentioned on their lists. (Generally group members are advised by the tour-leader to keep their baggage packed and ready for pick up outside their room doors at baggage down time).
6. The baggage from all rooms and floors is quietly collected and brought down to the lobby where it is neatly arranged in rows and stickers pasted on them.
7. The bell captain counts the baggage pieces.
8. The bell captain obtains a baggage out pass from the cashier and also collects any
9. keys that he may have collected from the tour members.
10. He hands over the keys to the reception where the receptionist scores out the room numbers of those rooms whose keys have been received. On the baggage out pass the receptionist mentions the numbers of rooms the keys of which have still to tender in the keys. The keys having been retrieved the baggage is loaded into the waiting tax's/Coaches as the case may be by the porters.
11. Though porters have been entrusted with the responsibility of collecting room keys from departing guests generally in a group departure this becomes slightly difficult. Therefore active assistance is rendered by the cashier, receptionist, room boy in collecting guest room keys and returning them to the reception before group check out.
12. Only one errand card is made, however numbers of all these porters who were engaged in group departure are mentioned on it.
13. An entry is made in the lobby attendant control sheet on dept.

Arrival of The Group
The procedure of Group arrival at the hotel varies from hotel to hotel but basically the following procedure is followed:

Activities concerning the group arrival start sometimes a few days before the arrival of the group when in the back office i.e. the Reservation office the Rooming list is typed. The Rooming list is the list which contains the names of all the members of the group with necessary details like their Names, Nationality, Passport details, etc. Some hotels even allocate the rooms to the various members of the groups and they are mentioned on the list, but this is possible only when all the necessary information like Name, Passport details, nationality, Types of rooms, Rooms configuration and sharing etc. are already provided by the Travel Agent in advance. (Rooming list Performa has already been given in Lesson Plan No. F.0.6.1 page 165 or the First Year Manual). Mail for the group (if any) is also sorted out. In some cases the rooms are blocked for the whole group (Blanket reservation) and the allocation of rooms is done only at the last minute when the guest arrives. Blanket reservation is done particularly when the members of the group arrive individually and not collectively. Then the rooms concerned are blocked on the Room Rack. Further since the group arrival generally involves the arrival of a large number of persons at the same time and the handling of their luggage various complications arise for the Front Office In charge He checks up from the Bell Desk that sufficient number of bell boys are available to handle the luggage of the whole group.

Key Envelopes

The keys of the rooms involved are then put in individual key envelopes along with meal coupons for the group members. The Key envelopes are marked with Room Numbers and the names of the Group members who are going to occupy those rooms on arrival. The pre-registration of the group is also done and after that the Room Key envelops. Rooming List and mail if any long with the pre-registered card are put in a special tray.

Group Arrival Counter

Many five star hotels who get a lot of group business have a special counter in the lobby to handle group arrivals. This helps the Front Office staff to concentrate on groups and work more efficiently: This also keeps the regular Front Desk uncrowned.

Welcome To Group

When the group arrives at the hotel, all the members are welcomed by some responsible Front Office staff like Lobby Manager, Front Office Manager or any other senior person. The group is also given the traditional Indian welcome by the P.R.O. department in the form of garland, aarti etc. The group members are then seated in the lobby and may be offered a welcome drink. Meanwhile the group leader is escorted to the special arrival counter. All the details about the group are reconfirmed with him. Later he is given the G.R. card which is already filled in to sign. (Depending upon the legal requirement either one card is prepared for the whole group and is signed by the group leader or individual cards may be required and signed by all the members of the group. In case only one card is made generally a Rooming list copy is attached with this. If the group members are of the same nationality, only one G.R. card is made, but if the group comprises of members with different nationalities then the number of G.R. cards will depend upon the total nationally break up of the group. After this the tray containing the Key envelopes, Rooming List, etc. is given to the group leader. He then distributes the key envelopes to the

While the group is registering, the luggage of the group is handled by the Bell Desk. This is a very important aspect. Generally when people travel in groups they are instructed by their group leader to put their name tags so that their luggage does not get mixed up. A copy of the Rooming list is also sent to the Bell Desk in advance. The bell boys then mark the luggage of the group members with the Room number allotted to them and transport the

After all the members have gone to their rooms and their luggage is delivered, the front desk staffs complete the following documents and activities.

The copies of the Rooming list fire circulated to the various departments like Lobby, Room Service, Reception, Housekeeping, telephone and group leader. A copy of the Rooming list is attached to the Registration Card. A 'C' form is also made for the group in case the group is a foreign group and a copy of the Rooming list is attached to the 'C' form

A Master Folio is then opened for the group and also individual Folios for each member of the group is made.

Group Departure

A Group Departure by and large is handled by all concerned sections of the Front Office in a fashion similar to the FIT departure, except that a team of page boys is engaged simultaneously in clearing guest baggage. The Stress is on co-ordination and efficiency and therefore a group's departure demands careful supervision. Elicited below are the slightly different and some special procedural steps that are to be borne in mind. These may be in addition to the regular procedure shown in the preceding pages.

At The Bell Desk

The Bell captain ensures sufficient staff is available in the shift.

- He checks the baggage down time and the wake call time of the group.
- Five minutes before baggage down timing, the bell captain allocates the floors and rooms to the page boys for bringing baggage down.
- The porters collect the baggage from rooms mentioned on their lists. (Generally group members are advised by the Tour leader to keep their baggage packed and ready for pick up outside their room doors at the baggage down time).
- The baggage from all rooms and floors is quietly collected and brought down to the lobby where it is neatly arranged in rows and stickers pasted on them.
- The Bell captain counts the baggage pieces.
- The Bell captain obtains a baggage out pass from the cashier after the tour leader settles down the bill, and ensures that keys from all the group members are retrieved.
- The keys are handed over to the Reception where the Receptionist scores out the room numbers of those rooms whose keys have been received, and after all keys arc received, the receptionist gives key clearance on the errand card.
- The Bell captain requests the Tour leader to count the baggage and also requests to contact those members of group who have not yet given their room key. The
- Though page boys/porters have been entrusted with the responsibility of collecting room keys from departing guests, generally in a group departure tills becomes slightly difficult, therefore active assistance is rendered by the Cashier, Receptionist, room boy in collecting guest room keys and returning them to the Receptionist before group leaves the hotel.
- Only one errand card is made, however numbers of all those porters / page boys who were engaged in group departure are mentioned on it. An entry is made in the Lobby attendant control sheet on departure.

At Reception

- The Reception issues a group departure notification about half an hour in advance of actual departure time to the Housekeeping, Room Service, Telephone Exchange and Coffee shop or Dining hall.

- On presentation of the baggage out pass / departure errand card of the group, Receptionist checks the receipt of Room keys by scoring out those rooms on the rooming list the keys of which have been received. The remainder room numbers are written on the baggage out pass/errand card to assist the bell captain in retrieving these keys.

At Cash Counter

- The Cashier takes out the group bill and the extra bill and calls the room service and coffee shop for any last minutes billing.
- Checks the complete bill and proceeds to update the bill.
- Takes out all extra's vouchers and separates them room wise and makes a small summary room wise to facilitate the cash collection.
- When the tour leader comes to the desk, he presents the main bill for approval. In the meantime a list of the rooms, who have to pay their extras is given to the Tour Leader.
- The Tour leader assists the cashier in collecting all extra charges from the tour members.
- After ratifying the bill the Tour leader is requested to sign the bill and the Hotel coupon or voucher duly signed is collected. This voucher is stapled on to the main bill noting down the following clearly and legibly in the appropriate column of the main bill.
  - ✓ Hotel coupon/vouchers no. and date.
  - ✓ Travel Agents Reference number.

Other Functions

The bell desk (Bell Boys) is called for performing many services which are not their scheduled one. In many cases they will have to go outside the hotel for such duties. Those can be treated as miscellaneous services.

Miscellaneous Services

1. Getting tickets for Cinema, Bus, Trains, and Airlines etc.
2. Going to the Post Office to buy Postage, to post the Hotel/Guest mail and to collect
3. Going to the Police Station and to Foreign Registration Office to give the C- Forms and Registration of guests.
4. Going to the Banks to deposit money/Foreign exchange etc.
5. In case of an emergency the bell boys will have to go to buy medicines etc.
6. Any other job which the situation may demand from time to time.

Procedure

First the bell captain will be informed by the appropriate authority. The Bell Captain will instruct the bell boy and he fills in a 'Service Call Slip' and the bell boy writes down the log book before he leaves the hotel. When the boy returns the time entered by the bell captain in the service call and signs it. This entry will be then transferred the bell captains control chart.

Front Office Communication

Communication is vital to FO operations because, nearly everything that happens in a hotel affects the FO in some way and vice versa. All functions of the front desk rely in part on clear communication. Effective communication is a pre-requisite to on efficient FO. Communication does not simply involve memorandums, face to face conversations and messages sent over the computer terminals. Effective FO communication also involves the use of log books, information directories, mail and telephone procedures. The larger the hotel, the larger and more complicated the communications network will be.

Log Book

The front desk may keep a log book so that all FO employees are aware of important events and decisions that occurred during previous work shifts. A typical FO log book is a journal which chronicles unusual events, guest complaints or request or relevant information. Front desk agents record notes in the log book during their shift, which should be clearly written in prescribed form so that they serve as a reference material for the next shift. Before beginning their shift, front desk agents should review and initial log book, noting any current activities, situations that require follow up or any potential problem. The employee must also note what action was taken. These, notations become an important link

Information Directory

FO personnel must be able to respond in a knowledgeable manner when guests contact the front desk for information. Common guest queries include:

- "Can you recommend a nearby restaurant?"
- "Can you arrange a taxi for me?"
- "Where is the shopping centre, drug store, petrol pump?"
- "How do I get the nearest bank with automated teller machine?"
- "Where is the theater, stadium, and where can I get the tickets?"
- "When is the check out time?"
- "How do I get the university, library or the museum?"
- "Where is the district court?"
- "What recreational facilities are available in the hotel or near the hotel?"

Front desk agents may need to acquire rather obscure information to answer certain questions of guests. Some properties accumulate such data in a bound guide called INFORMATION DIRECTORY. This may include simplified maps of the area, taxi and airline company contact addresses and telephone numbers, banks, theaters, churches, store locations and special events schedules. Front desk agents should be familiar with the information directory and know how to use it as reference.

Some hotels have installed computer information terminals in public areas. These are essentially an electronic equivalent of the front desk information directory. Since these arc easily accessed by the guests without employee assistance, their use often release front desk agents to attend other guest needs. A close circuit television system can also reduce the volume information requested at the front desk.

Mail Handling

Registered guests rely on the FO to deliver mail quickly and efficiently. In general, hotels time stamp all guest mails when it arrives at the property. Doing so provides evidence of when the mail was received, incase any question arises on how promptly the mail was delivered. When mail arrives, FO records should always be checked immediately to see if the guest is either registered, due to check-in, or has checked out. Different mail handling procedures will be followed in each instance.

Usually mail for a registered guest is held in the appropriate room's slot in a mail and message rack. The front desk should notify a guest as soon as possible that he or she has received mail. Some properties do this by switching on an in-room message light on the guest room telephone. Others deliver a printed form to the guest room. If the mail arrives for a guest who has not yet checked in, a notation should be made on the guest reservation form and the mail held until the guest arrives. Quest mail that has not been picked up or has arrived for a guest who has already checked out, should be time stamped a second time and

Guest may also received registered letters, express mail packages requiring a signature on delivery. Some hotels permit the front desk agent to sign for such mail. After doing so the agent records the items delivered in a log and has the guest sign a signature book at the

Telephone Services

Most hotels provide in-room local and long distance telephone service 24 hours a day. Regardless of whether front desk agent or telephone operators answer in-coming calls, all employees answering calls should be courteous and helpful. Telephone messages recorded by FO personnel should be time stamped and placed in the guest's mail and message rack slot. If the guest room telephones are equipped with message indicator light, the front desk may switch on the in-room message light so that guest knows that a message is waiting for him at the front desk.

Voice Mail

Voice mail is the newest technology in the area of guest mail and message service. Voice mail boxes are devices which can record messages for guest. A caller wishes to leave any message for a guest simply speaks into the phone. His/her message is then recorded by the voice mail box system. To retrieve the message, the guest typically dials a special telephone number which connects him / her with the voice mail box and listens to the message.

Facsimiles

Fax messages are usually treated like the telephone message. FO personnel generally stamp fax messages received at the property, which are kept in guest's mail or message rack. The guests are notified according to the procedure of the hotel. Some hotels keep a log of every fax received. Information recorded in the fax log book may list the recipient, the sender, the time the fax was received and the total number of pages. A similar record is kept of outgoing faxes if the property offers such a service. If it is undelivered, the hotel should record immediately notify the party sending fax. Many hotels charge guests for receiving faxes.

Wake Up Services

Front desk agents must pay special attention to wake up call requests. FO computer systems can be used to remind front desk agents to place wake up calls be programmed to place the calls and play a recorded wake up message. Despite advances in technology, many hotels still prefer that front desk agents place wake up calls, since the guest appreciates the

The front desk is responsible for coordinating guest services. Typical guest services involve providing information and special equipment and supplies. Quest services may also include accommodating guests through specials procedures. A guest's satisfaction at the hotel partly depends on the ability of the front desk to respond to a request.

A growing number of hotels employ a concierge or other designated stuff member to handle guest request. A concierge embodies the warmth and hospitality of the entire property. As more hotel functions become automated, the concierge may become more and more important for re-enforcing the hotel's personal touch In guest services.

Interdepartmental Communications

Many services in a hotel require coordination between the front office and other departments or divisions. The front office generally exchanges the most information with personnel in house keeping and in engineering and maintenance. From desk agents should also recognize how they can influence the performance of the hotel's revenue centers through the use of marketing and public relations skills.

Housekeeping

Housekeeping and the front office must keep each other informed of changes in rooms' status to ensure that guests are roomed efficiently and without complications. The more familiar front office personnel are with housekeeping procedures - and vice versa - the smoother the relationship will be between the two departments.

Engineering and Maintenance

In many hotels, engineering and maintenance personnel begin each shift by examining the front desk log book for repair work orders. Front desk agents use the log book to track maintenance problems reported by guests or staff; such as poor heating or cooling, faulty plumbing, noisy equipment; or broken furniture. The log book can serve as an excellent reference for the hotel's engineering and maintenance staff.

Many hotels use a multiple-part work order form to report maintenance problems. Exhibit 6.2 shows a sample maintenance work order form. When the work is completed, the engineering and maintenance division informs the department that filed the work request order. If a maintenance problem makes a room unsaleable, the front office must know immediately when the problem is fixed so the room can be placed back in available inventory. This *minimizes* the revenue lost through out-of-order guestrooms. To enhance hotel operations, some hotels employ engineering and maintenance staffs round the clock.

Revenue Centers

Although hotels enjoy their greatest revenues through guest room sales, additional services and activities may support a hotel's profitability. In addition to the rooms division, hotel revenue centers may include :

- ❖ Coffee shops, snack bars, and specialty restaurants
- ❖ Gift shops, barber shops, and newsstands
- ❖ Banquet, meeting, and catering facilities
- ❖ Local and long-distance telephone service
- ❖ Health clubs, golf courses, and exercise rooms
- ❖ Car rentals, limousine services, and tours
- ❖ Valet parking and parking garages.

Guests frequently learn about these services and facilities through a printed directory placed in each guest room. Front desk agents must also be familiar with these facilities and services so thy can answer guest questions in a positive and knowledgeable way. The transactions charged by guests at hotel restaurants, gift shops and other remote points of sale must be communicated to the front desk to ensure eventual payment.

Marketing And Public Relations

The front office should be among the first to know about events the hotel schedules for publicity. In many ways, a hotel's marketing and public relations effort depends on the participation and enthusiasm of front office personnel. Guest receptions, health and fitness programs, family events and even complimentary coffee in a hotel's lobby may provide settings for guests to socialize and can promote repeat business. Front office personnel may contribute to hotel newsletters, guest history systems, and customized registration and checkout processes that help personalize hotel services for frequent guests.

Front Office Security

Providing security in a hotel means protecting people - guests, employees, and others and assets. Because the diversity of the lodging industry makes national security standards infeasible, each lodging property or chain must develop its own security program. Each hotel's security program should meet the hotel's own particular needs. The responsibility for developing and maintaining a property's security program lies with its management. The information presented here is intended only as an introduction, and only includes those elements relevant to the front office. Hotel management should consult legal counsel to ensure that the property is in compliance with applicable laws.

The Security Department of A Hotel is Responsible For The Following Areas of Concern:

These operational procedures arc never really appreciated until a crime occurs or a disaster strikes a hotel. They arc assumed to be in place but somehow seem to take a backseat to meeting the immediate needs and financial objectives of the organization:

Organization of a Security Department

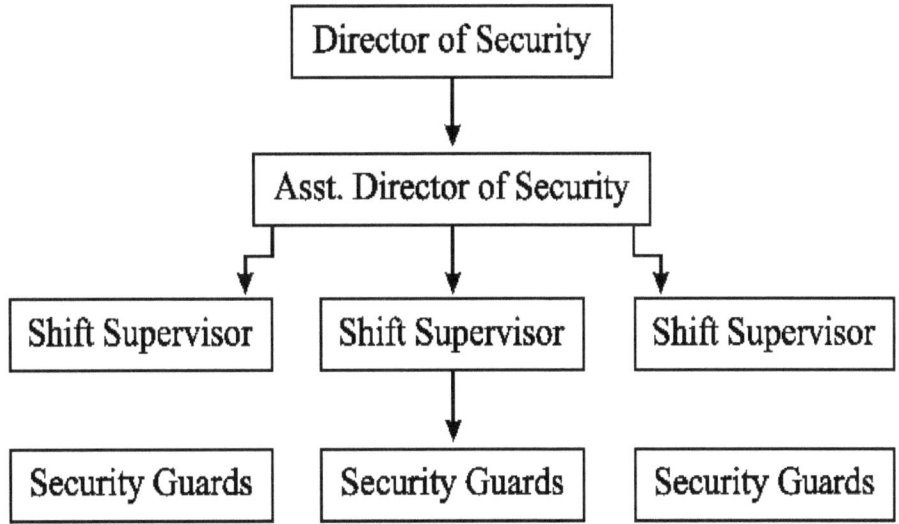

The security director needs personnel, technology and a budget to operate a 24-hr control system for the hotel. Depending on the size of the hotel, there may be an asst, director of security, who assist in the administrative and supervisory functions of the dept

Importance of Security Department

The Front Office is a hotel's communication center, it is a vital link between the hotel management and the guest. In case of any emergency, the guest calls up Front Office. The staff of Front Office on duty cannot leave and resolve the emergency because they must continue to provide communication services and process financial transactions. The security department staff must react with speed and efficiency to serve the guest.

The security department is a very active dept, setting policies, organizing programs and delivering training programs to promote guest and employee safety. The Director of Security is a trained professional who must ensure that a busy hotel filled with guests, employees and equipment remains safe. One of the dept's goals is to prevent emergencies through planning. Another goal is to train all hotel employees for emergencies when they

The Role of the Front Office

A security program is most effective when all employees participate in the hotel's security efforts. Front office personnel play a particularly important role from desk agents, door attendants, bell persons, and parking attendants have the opportunity to observe all the people who arrive at or depart from the premises. Suspicious activities or circumstances involving a guest or a visitor can be reported to the hotel's security department or a

For example, front desk agents should never give keys, room numbers, messages, or mail to anyone asking for them without first seeing appropriate identification. The front desk agent should not announce an arriving guest's room number.

Guests may be further protected if the hotel prohibits staff members from providing guest information to callers or visitors. Generally, front desk agents should not give out guestroom numbers. People calling guests at the hotel may be directly connected to the appropriate guestroom without being told the room number. Those inquiring in person about a guest may be asked to use the house phone to call the guestroom.

Front office employees may also inform guests of personal precautions they may take. For example, front desk agents may suggest that guests Hide and secure any valuables in their cars if they drove to the property. Bell persons accompanying the guest to a room generally provide instructions on the operation of room equipment. The bell person may also review the use of access control devices on the guest room doors and windows familiarize the guest with pertinent security information, and point out any decals or notices in the room relating to guest security.

A hotel also helps protect its guests' personal property. The front office may develop a method for ensuring the safety and security of the luggage of arriving guests. Often, luggage and other articles received by a door attendant are move to. a secured area; guests later recover their belongings by presenting a receipt. Other hotel employees can assist in protecting the guests' property. A valet puking attendant, for example, should secure all parked vehicle keys so that they cannot be removed by anyone except authorized employees.

Front office personnel are also important players in asset protection. Failure to collect payment from guests is usually amore significant loss that, for instance, the theft of towels or ashtrays.

In-House Security Department versus Contracted Security Service

The GM of a hotel must determine if operating an in-house security dept is cost-effective. Operating a well organized security dept must be the primary concern when considering the hiring of an outside security agency.

Foot patrol, walking the halls, corridors and outside the hotel to detect breaches of guest and employee safety, is an important feature of security, but it is a preventive measure, not an active means of organizing security. In some cases the GM will be forced for economic reasons, to hire an outside service. Administrative and planning procedures for operating a security are delegated to other department heads. The cost consideration must be weighed against planning and coordinating a safe environment for the guest and

Escort service, a uniformed security guard escorting a hotel employee to a bank to make deposits, for performing regular hall patrol and for maintaining surveillance of the parking garage may seem cost effective if outside agency is engaged compared to salaries and administrative overhead incurred by operating an in-house security department. But more than cost must be considered. The implementing of fire safety and security procedures, delivering of fire safety and security training sessions, monitoring fire safety devices, updating management on the latest technology to ensure a safe environment- who will supervise and control these aspects of security?

If an outside security service is hired, the role of maintaining security is parceled out to the various dept heads. The Maintenance head will operate the fire safety and security equipment and react to hazardous situations. The GM will if time permits establish a safety committee. Under these circumstances, safety and security become low priorities. The lack of coordination almost guarantees disaster when an emergency strikes.

The challenges of crime prevention education and training to providing security to guests and employees require a full-time approach to fulfill this responsibility. Directors of security have been assigned new duties such as risk management and liaison with the police. Part-time efforts to control crisis in a hotel may be short sighted.

Key Control

For security reasons, most lodging properties used at least three types of guestroom keys: emergency keys, master keys, and individual guestroom keys. An emergency key open all guestroom doors, even when they are double-locked - that is, locked with both a standard door lock and a device operable only from within the guestroom. Emergency keys should be operable only from within the guestroom. Emergency keys should be highly protected. Their use should be strictly controlled and recorded. An emergency key should never be taken from the hotel property.

A master key opens all guestrooms that are not double-locked. When not in use on the property, a master key should be secured in a designated place for safekeeping. Only authorized personnel should have access to master keys. Keys are issued to personnel based on their need to use the key - not simply on their status. A written record should be maintained of which employees have received a master key.

A guestroom key opens a single guestroom if the door is not double-locked. Front desk agents should not give a guestroom key to just anyone; who asks for the key is the guest registered to that room. In addition, front desk agents should remind guests to return keys at checkout. Additional reminders include well-secured key return boxes in the lobby, at hotel exits, and in courtesy vehicles. Some properties have reduced key loss by requiring a key deposit from each guest at registration. Key deposits also help to bring the guest back to the front desk before he or she leaves - which can contribute to the effective settlement of a guest account. The front desk should work closely with engineering and maintenance to assure that guestrooms are re-keyed periodically. Hotels have been held liable for the theft of guest items from guestrooms because they failed to change door locks. Most new mechanical key systems are designed for frequent replacement of keys.

Some properties do not list their name, address, or room numbers on guestroom keys. Then, if a guestroom key is lost and falls into the wrong hands, it cannot be traced to the property for criminal use. A code number is typically stamped on the key in place of the room number; a master code list is maintained at the front desk.

Regardless of their responsibilities or position, employees should never take hotel keys from the property. Many organizations require that all keys should be returned to security and placed in a locked cabinet in a secured area of the property. Keys issued on a temporary basis should be recorded in a log. The log should indicate the reason for issue, issue date, time out, time in, recipient's name, and issuer's name. Whenever there is any known or suspected compromise of a key, an unauthorized entry by key, or any loss or theft, very lock affected should be changed or rotated to another part of the property.

Electronic Locking Systems

electronic locking system replaces traditional mechanical locks with sophisticated computer-based guestroom access devices. A centralized electronic locking system operates through a master control console at the front desk, which is wired to every guestroom door, registration, a front desk agent inserts a key or card into the appropriate room slot on the to transmit its code to the guestroom door lock. The key or card, issued to the guest, the only working guestroom key.

Centralized electronic locking system presents an additional opportunity for improved , and helps reduce employee theft. Many of these systems keep track of which keys cards opened which doors - by date, and by time. If the hotel staff knows about the system's capability, employees tempted to steal may think twice since they realize the entry may incriminate them. Report creation and other system functions should be controlled by operator identification and password security codes.

Unlike the centralized system, a micro-fitted electronic locking system operates on an individual unit basis. Each door has its own microprocessor which contains a predetermined sequence of codes. A master console at the front desk contains a record of all code sequences stored within each guestroom door. At registration, the front desk agent encodes a key or card with the next code in the sequence for the assigned room the console and each microprocessor must agree on which code in the sequence is currently valid. These types of locking systems don't require the extensive computer hardware that centralized systems do which can make them an affordable option for small properties.

Most electronic locking systems provide several distinct levels of security, parallel to the levels of keying in traditional systems. Systems may include various guest safety and convenience features, such as a do not disturb signal. One form of electronic locking system does not require keys or cards at all; guests set the locking mechanism by programming their own four-digit code numbers, or by using their personal (magnetic stripe) credit card.

Surveillance And Access Control

Although open to the public, a hotel is a private property. An innkeeper has the responsibility to monitor and, when appropriate, to control the activities of people on the premises. All employees should be trained to watch for suspicious people and situations. Surveillance plays a role in most aspects of guest and property protection. Discouraging suspicious or unauthorized individuals from entering the property relies in part On procedures for responding to the observations of employees.

Most lobbies are set up so the front desk agent can see the property's entrances, elevator, escalators, and stairways. Mirrors may be placed in strategic locations to aid visibility. Observing escalators is important for both security and safety reasons; personnel should know how to stop the escalators in an emergency.

In many hotels, someone is stationed at the front desk at all times. In a small property, a front desk agent may be the only staff member on the premises during late night hours. Under such circumstances, some properties limit access to the lobby and reception area, and give the front desk agent the authority to deny admittance. If the front desk agent needs to leave the desk area for any reason, many properties advise the agent to lock the front door. This way, no once can enter the hotel until the gent returns to the front desk.

Successful surveillance techniques typically rely on hotel personnel. Proper equipment, however, can enhance many surveillance functions. Closed-circuit television can be an effective surveillance tool in multiple-entry properties. Usually, monitors are located in a control center. Employees are assigned to watch the monitors and respond to incidents picked up by surveillance cameras.

Surveillance equipment is intended to help employees, not replace them. An elevator may be equipped and programmed to stop at a certain floor for observation, but it is still up to personnel to actually do the observing. Likewise, a closed-circuit television system is a worthless security device without people monitoring it.

Protection of Funds

The accounting division is primarily responsible for the protection of hotel funds. However, other departments, particularly the front office contribute by protecting certain financial assets.

The front desk cashiering function plays a critical role in the protection of hotel funds. The amount of cash in a cash register should be limited through a cash bank system. At the start of each work shift, each cashier is given the smallest amount of cash that will allow him or her to transact business normally. The cashier is responsible for this cash bank and for all cash added to it during the work shift. Ideally, only one person should have access to each cash bank, and each bank should be in a separate cash drawer.

All transactions should be recorded immediately. The cashier should close the cash register drawer after each transaction. A cashier working with an pen cash register drawer may fail to record a transaction, either accidentally or deliberately. Cashiers should complete any transaction in process before changing currency into different denominations for guests; each change requests should be handled as a new transaction to avid confusion. A supervisor or a member of the accounting division should occasionally conduct an unscheduled audit of front office cash registers.

The hotel should have a policy that states where employees should place cash during a transaction. Generally, the employee should not place currency on the cash register ledge.

This can make it easy for a thi :f to grab the money and run. Some organisations recommend that the money be placed in (the cash drawer, but above the clip until the transaction is completed. This helps to prevent any disputes over what denomination and

Safe Custody of Guest Valuables

The hotelier has a liability towards the property of a guest and he is obliged to accept articles such as jewelry, cash, etc for safekeeping. The hotel can either accept articles from the guest for safekeeping or can provide facilities like lockers where the guest can keep his valuables. The hotel has to display a notice informing the guest about the safekeeping facilities in a prominent place where it can be noticed by the guest. The hotelier must also inform the guest about these facilities orally. Once he has accepted the responsibility for the safely of the guest valuables, the guest can clam damages for the following:

1. The property was lost or damaged in spite of the fact that they were given for safekeeping.
2. The hotel refused to accept guest's valuables for safekeeping and later they were lost on. stolen.
3. The hotel failed to display a notice in a prominent place and the guest was not aware of this facility.

Procedure

1. Common Safe

When a guest deposits his valuables for safe custody, he is given a specially prepared envelope in which he puts the articles. He seals the envelope and signs across it. The cashier gives a receipt for the envelope. The receipts are serially numbered and are in triplicate. Top copy is given to the guest, second copy is attached to the envelope and the third copy is the book copy. A deposit register is also maintained in which the details of the receipt arc posted.

When the guest requests for the return of the property, he gives back the original of the receipt. This is cancelled and is attached to the third copy in the book. The deposit receipt book is checked against the deposit register to ensure that all deposits have been entered in the register and all the receipts are returned to the book after returning the guest article.

2. Individual Safe Deposit Lockers

As the above process is time consuming and could lead to confusion, mostly individual safe deposit lockers are used. When valuables are to be deposited the guest is given the key of the locker, which he signs for and the particulars are recorded in the 'Safe deposit locker record sheet'. There are two keys for each locker. When the locker has to be opened both the keys have to be used. The cashier is responsible for the control key and the second key is the guest key. The cashier uses his key and then guest can open the locker with his key. This prevents the guest or the staff from tampering with the lockers. The front desk must verify the identity of the guest before granting him the access to the safe deposit box. The guest is required to sign a form requesting the access to the locker and the staff will verify the signature with the guest signature on the safe deposit locker form. A few hotels also take a deposit for the key. It is refunded at the time of departure on production of the key receipt.

In some hotels safe deposit lockers are also placed in the guest rooms. In- room safes are generally placed in the guest room closet or wardrobe. Guest convenience is the main advantage of the in-room safe. Several different types of in-room safe systems exist. A few of them have mechanical locks while others have electronic locks that can be coded by the guests. Every guest slaying in the room can lock the safe with his own code and the guest is requested to leave the safe open when he checks out.

In case a guest does not remember the code, he can take help from the hotel security officers who have a master key that will open the safe.

Guest Services

As the center of front office activity, the front-desk is responsible for coordinating guest services. Typical guest services involve providing information and special equipment and supplies. Guest services may also include accommodating guests through special procedures. A guest's satisfaction at the hotel hinges in part on the ability of the font desk to respond to a request. A request that falls beyond his responsibility of the front office should be referred to the appropriate person or department.

A growing number of hotels employ a concierge or other designated staff member to handle guest requests. A concierge embodies the warmth and hospitality of the entire property. As more hotel functions become automated, the concierge may become even more important for reinforcing the hotel's personal touch in guest services.

Guests may request special equipment and supplies while making a reservation, at the time of registration, or during occupancy. Reservations agents should have a reliable method of recording special requests to ensure that they are properly met. When a guest needs special equipment or supplies, he or she will almost always ask a front desk agent. The front desk agent, in turn, follows through by contacting the appropriate service center or hotel department. Equipment and supplies commonly requested by guests include:

- Additional clothes hangers
- Audiovisual equipment
- Special equipment for blind, physically handicapped or hearing impaired guests

Four desk agents should have alternative ways to meet guest requests when the department that normally provides the equipment or service is closed or inaccessible. Housekeeping, for example, attends to many guest requests, but may not be staffed around the clock. In some hotels, front office personnel may have access to linen rooms during late night hours. In others, the housekeeping department may stock a centrally located linen closet and give a key to appropriate front office personnel. This technique enables the front office staff to satisfy requests for additional linen and pillows even when the housekeeping department is closed.

Special Procedures

Guests may ask for special treatment when making a reservation, registering at the front desk, checking out - or for that matter, during any point of their stay. Sometimes, these special requests represent exceptions to standard front office procedures. Reservations agents should have a reliable method of recording special requests made during the reservations process and communicating them to appropriate front office personnel. Front desk agents should also have a way to record any procedural requests they handle.

Procedural requests may require more time and effort to fulfill than equipment and supply requests. Typical procedural requests include:

- Split account folios Master account folios
- Wake-up calls
- Transportation arrangements
- Entertainment reservations
- Newspaper delivery
- Secretarial services

A knowledgeable front desk agent usually can fulfill a special request involving guest folios. Business travellers most often request split folio. Essentially, these folios separate guest charges onto two or more separate folios. One folio account may be set up to record room and tax charges, this part of the folio may be billed to the guest's company. Another folio account may be set up to track incidental charges such as telephone calls, food, and the beverages; this part of the folio will most likely be paid directly by the guest.

A convention group meeting in the hotel may request a master folio. Typically, only the charges incurred by the group are posted to the master folio and billed to the sponsoring agent. Each group member is response ble for other charges posted to his or her individual folio account. The purpose of a master folio is to collect authorized charges not

Concierges may handle other procedural requests. Hotels without a concierge may have front desk agents update and use the information directory as a resource for referrals and outside services.

Guest Relations

Despite staff efficiency and attentiveness, guests will occasionally be disappointed or find fault with something or someone. Hotels should anticipate guest complaints and devise strategies that help staff effectively resolve the situation.

The high visibility of the front office means front desk agents are frequently the first to learn of guest complaints. Front desk agents should be especially attentive to guests with complaints and seek a satisfactory resolution to the problem. Nothing annoys guests more than having their complaints ignored, discounted, or overlooked. While most front office staff do not enjoy receiving complaints, they should understand that very few guests actually enjoy complaining. Employees should also realize that guests who do not have the opportunity to complain to hotel staff often tell their friends, relatives and business associates instead.

When guests find it easy to express their opinions, both the hotel and the guests benefit. The hotel learns of potential or actual problems and has the opportunity to resolve them. For a guest, this means a more satisfying stay; when problems arc resolved, a guest often feels that the hotel cares about his or her needs. From this perspective, every complaint should be welcomed as an opportunity to enhance guest relations. Guests who leave a hotel dissatisfied may never return.

Complaints

Guest complaints can be divided into four categories of problems; mechanical, attitudinal, service-related, and unusual.

Most guest complaints relate to hotel equipment malfunctions. Mechanical complaints usually concern problems with climate control, lighting, electricity, room furnishings, ice machines, vending machines, door keys, plumbing, television sets, elevator, and so on. Even an excellent preventive maintenance program cannot completely eliminate all potential equipment problems. Effective use of a front desk log book and maintenance work orders may help reduce the frequency of mechanical complaints.

Guests may make attitudinal complaints when they feel insulted by rude or tactless hotel staff members. Guests who overhear staff arguments or who receive complaints from staff members may also make attitudinal complaints. Guests should not overhear employees arguing or become sounding boars for employee problems. Managers and supervisor should hear and attend to the complaints and problems of staff - not guests. This is especially critical to maintaining sound guest relations.

Guests may make service related- complaints when they experience a problem with service. These complaints can be wide-ranging and can be made about such things as long waits for service, lack of assistance with luggage, untidy rooms, phone difficulties, missed wake-up calls, cold or ill-prepared food, or ignored requests for additional supplies. A hotel generally receives more service-related complaints when it is operation at or near full occupancy.

Guests may also complain about the absence of a swimming pool, lack of public transportation, bad weather, and so on. Hotel generally has little or no control over the circumstances surrounding unusual complaints. Nonetheless, guests sometimes expect the hotel to resolve such situations. Front office mangers should alert front desk agents that some guests will complain about things they can do nothing about. This way, staff will be prepared to handle the situation through appropriate guest relations techniques - and avoid a potentially difficult encounter.

Identifying Complaints

All guest complaints deserve attention, even though they differ in nature and importance. An excited guest complaining loudly at the front desk requires immediate attention. A guest making an offhand comment deserves no less attention - although the need for action may be less immediate.

Guest relations stand to improve when a hotel systematically identifies its most frequent guest complaints. By reviewing a properly kept front desk long book, management can often identify and address recurring complaints and problems.

Another way to identify complaints involves the evaluation of guest comment cards or questionnaires. Guest questionnaires may be distributed at the front desk, placed conspicuously in the guestroom or mailed to guests following departure.

Identifying problems is one of the first steps in taking corrective action. By examining the number and type of complaints receive, hotel management may gain insight into common and leas common problems. Front office staff members may be better equipped to handle frequent complaints courteously and effectively, especially if they know the problem cannot be immediately corrected.

Handling Complaints

It is usually counterproductive to ignore a guest complaint. In many hotels, front desk agents are instructed to refer complaints to supervisors or managers. But sometimes, front desk agents may not be able to pass the complaint on - especially when the complaint demands immediate attention. Hotels should have a contingency plan in place for such.

The front desk may receive complains about food and beverage operations in the hotel, regardless of whether those operations are managed by the hotel. Unless the hotel and the food and beverage operators establish procedures for referring complaints, guests may continue to be upset and the hotel Will continue to receive the blame. The hotel and its revenue outlets should maintain close communications and develop procedures designed to

Managers and employees should keep these points in mind when handling guest

- ❖ Guests may be quite angry. Staff members should never go along to a guestroom to investigate a problem or otherwise risk potential danger.
- ❖ Staff members should never make a promise that exceeds their authority.
- ❖ If a problem cannot be solved, staff members should admit this early On. Honesty is the best policy.
- ❖ Some guests complain as part of their nature, and may never be satisfied. The front office should develop an approach for dealing with such guests.

Learning to deal effectively with complaints requires experience. Front office staff members can practice by thinking about how they might resolve some of the hotel's most common complaints. Role-playing can also be an effective method in learning to deal with complaints. By anticipating complaints, planning and practicing responses, and receiving constructive feedback, staff members should be better prepared to deal with guest complaints.

Follow-Up Procedures

Management may use the front desk log book to initiate corrective action, verify that complaints have been resolved and identify recurring problems. This comprehensive written record may also enable management to contact guests who are still dissatisfied at checkout. A letter from the front office manager expressing regret about the incident is usually sufficient to promote goodwill and demonstrate concern for guest satisfaction. Some, managers may telephone checked-out guests to get a more complete picture of the incident, depending on its significance. Chain hotels may also receive guest complaints channeled through chain headquarters. Cumulative records of complaints about each hotel in the chain may be compiled and sent regularly to managers. This method of feedback allows the chain's corporate headquarters to evaluate and compare each hotel's guest relations

Checkout And Settlement Process

Checkout and settlement processes are part of final stage of the guest cycle. The services and activities of the departure stage are primarily furnished by the front office employee - be it a front desk agent, front desk cashier or both. Personnel in the accounting division may be involved as well. Before living the hotel the guest will generally stop at the front desk to review his or her folio, pay any outstanding account balance, receive a receipt of his or her account statement and return the room key.

Many guests will forget all the previous courteousness and hard work of the hotel staff if checkout and settlement do not go smoothly.

Functions of Checkout And Settlement

The functions of checkout and settlement process accomplish three very important

Update Room Status Information

Guest account settlement depends on an affective front office accounting system that maintains accurate guest folio, verifies and authorizes a method of settlement and resolves discrepancies in account balance. Generally the front office finds it most affective to settle a guest account while the guest is still in the hotel. A guest can settle an account by paying cash, charging the balance to a credit card, differing payment to an approved direct billing or using a combination of the payment methods.

Most front office requires a guest to specify an eventual method of settlement at the time of registration. This means that the front office will know that the guest credit card or direct billing information before he or she arrives at the desk to checkout. Such notification allows the front office to verify and authorize a credit card account or confirm a direct billing in advance of the settlement Pre-settlement verification activity reduces the guest's checkout time and improves the front office ability to conduct outstanding account balance.

Affective front office operation depends on accurate room rate status information. When a guest checkout and settles his account, the front desk perform several important tasks.

First, the agent changes the guest room status from occupied to an on change on the room status report. On change is a housekeeping term that means that the guest has left the hotel and that the room he occupied needs to be cleaned and readied for the next guest. After making the room status change the front desk notifies the housekeeping department that the guest has departed.

In hotels with manual or semi automated systems the front desk communicates information to the housekeeping by telephone or through an electronic room status board. In hotels with fully automated property management system information is relayed automatically when the front desk agent changes the room status from occupied to on change.

A housekeeper then cleans and readies the room for inspection and resale. To maximize room sale the front office must maintain a current occupancy and housekeeping status of all rooms.

The hotel can better understand it's cliental and determine guest trends when it maintains a guest history file. A guest history file is a collection of personal and financial data about guests who have stayed in the hotel. An individual guest history record within the file normally contains personal and transactional information relevant to the guest stay. The front office may create guest history file from expired registration card or through sophisticated computer based system, which automatically directs guest checkout information in to a guest history database. Guest history file provides a powerful database for strategic marketing.

Departure Procedure

Checkout and settlement can be a pleasant experience when the front office is well prepared and organized. This final phase of guest cycle involves several steps designed to accomplish checkout and settlement in a systematic manner.

1. Inquiring about addition recent charges.

2. Updating the room status.

Checkout and settlement procedures vary from property to property based on the level of service and degree of automation.

The amount of face-to-face contact between the guest and front desk personnel may also vary since some hotel offer special automated or express checkout service. Despite such variations checkout and settlement represents an essential front office responsibility.

Like check-in, checkout gives the hotel an opportunity to make a positive impression on the guest. The guest approaching the front desk should be greeted promptly. To prevent any messages or mail going unclaimed the front desk agent should check for any messages or mail awaiting guest pick-up. To ensure the guest folio is accurate and complete the front desk agent should process any outstanding charges that need posting. In addition the agent should ask the guest if he or she incurred any recent charges and make necessary adjustments to the guest folio.

The guest receives a final copy of his or her account folio at checkout At this time the front desk agent should verify exactly how the guest intends to settle his or her account regardless of which settlement method the guest specified at registration. This is necessary because many hotels require guest to establish credit at check-in, no matter how they plan to settle at the checkout. A guest may establish credit by presenting a credit card and then decide to settle his or her account by cash.

After determining how the guest will pay the front desk agent should then bring the guest account balance to zero. This is typically called "Zeroing out the account". The guest account balance must be settled in full for an account to be considered zeroed out. Guest account, which are zeroed out at the time of the departure are transferred to the city ledger for billing and collection by the accounting department.

Method of Settlement

A guest account can be zeroed out in several ways:

1. Cash Payment in Full

A cash payment in full at checkout will bring a guest account balance to zero. A front desk agent should mark the folio as paid. A guest may have had a credit card imprinted at registration even though he or she intends to settle his or her account by cash. The front desk agent should destroy any credit card vouchers imprinted at registration when the guest pays in full with cash.

Credit card settlement creates a transfer credit on the guest folio and moves the account balance from the guest ledger to the credit card account in the city ledger.

Like credit card settlement direct billing transfers the account balance from the guest ledger to the city ledger. Unlike credit card settlement, responsibility for billing and collecting the direct billing is the hotels, rather then an outside agency. Direct billings are not normally an acceptable method of settlement unless the billing has been arranged and approved by the hotel before or during guest registration. To complete a direct billing settlement a front desk agent should have the guest sign the folio to verify that the postings are correct and that he or she accepts all charges listed on the folio for collection.

2. Combined Settlement Method

A guest may use more than one settlement method to zero put a folio balance. For example, the guest may make partial cash payment and charge the remainder of his or her account balance to a credit card. Front desk agent must accurately record the combined settlement method and ensure that all required paperwork is properly completed.

Late Checkout

Guest do not always checkout by the hotels posted checkouts, hotel should post checkout time notices in places, such as on the back of. the guestroom door and at the front desk. A reminder of checkout time can also be included in any pre departure material distributed to the guest.

Some hotels authorize a front desk to charge late checkout fees. A guest will probably be surprised to see such a fee on the folio if he or she is not familiar with the hotels policy. Whenever guest calls a front desk and requests a late checkout, the front desk employee should inform the guest about any additional charges.

Express Checkout

Guest sometimes encounters long lines at front desk before 7:30 am and 12 noon, a prime checkout period for many guests. To ease front office pressure some properties initiate checkout activity before the guest is actually ready to leave. A common pre-departure activity involves producing and distributing guest folio to guest expected to checkout in the morning.

Front office staff may quickly slip printed folios under the guestroom door before 6 am making sure that the guest folio cannot be seen or reached from the outside.

Normally the front office will distribute an express checkout form with the predeparture folio. Express checkout may include a note requesting the guest to notify the front desk if departure plans change. Otherwise the front office will assume the guest is leaving by the hotel posted checkout time. This procedure usually encourages guest to quickly notify the front office of any changes in departure before the hotels checkout time.

By completing such a form the guest transfers his or her outstanding folio balance to the credit card voucher that was created at registration. The guest then deposits the express checkout form at the front desk at the time of departure. After the guest leaves the front office must complete the guest checkout by transferring the outstanding guest folio balance to a previously authorized method of settlement. Any additional charges the guest makes before leaving the hotel (For example, telephone calls) will be added to his or her folio before the front desk agent zeros out the account. Because of this the amount due on the guests copy of the express checkout folio may not match the charges posted to his or her credit card. This possibility should be clearly stated on the express checkout form to avoid confusion later on.

Self-Checkout

In some properties guest can check themselves out by accessing self-checkout terminal in the lobby or by using in room system. Self-checkout terminal and in room system are interfaced with the front office computer and are intended to reduce checkout time and front office traffic. Self-checkout terminal vary in design. Some resemble an automatic bank teller machine, while the other possesses video and audio capabilities. To use a self-checkout terminal the guest accesses the proper folio and reviews its contents. Guest may require to enter a credit card number by using a keypad or by inserting the credit card in the machine. Settlement can be automatically assigned to a credit card as long as the guest presents a valid card at registration.

Checkout is complete when the guest balance is posted to a credit card account and an itemized account statement is printed and dispensed to the guest. The self-checkout system then automatically communicates the updated room status to the front office computer. The system also relays information and instructions for updating or creating a guest history record.

Unpaid Account Balances

No matter how carefully the font office monitors the guest's stay, there is always the possibility that a guest will leave without settling his or her account. Some guests may honestly forget to check out. The front office may also discover late charges after a guest has checked out. Other guests may leave the hotel with no intention of settling their account. The guests are commonly referred to as skippers. Regardless of the reason, after-departure charges or balances represent unpaid account balances. Late charges may be major concern in guest account settlement. A late charge is a transaction requiring posting to a guest account that does not reach the front office until after the guest has checked out and closed the account. Restaurant, telephone, and room service charges are examples of potential late charges. Since the guest may not pay for these purchases before leaving, the hotel may never collect for the transactions. Even if late charges are eventually paid, the hotel incurs the additional Costs involved in billing the guest. Sometimes, the extra expenses for labor, postage, stationery and special statement forms may total more than the amount of the late charge. Few hotels can afford a large volume of late charges. Reducing late charges is important to maximizing profitability. From desk agents can take several steps to help reduce the occurrence of late charges.

- ❖ Post transactional vouchers as soon as they arrive at the front desk. This procedure will help minimize the volume of un-posted charges during the check-out period.

- ❖ Survey front office equipment for un-posted charges before checking a guest out. For example, telephone traffic monitors and in-room movie charge meters possess transactional information but may not be voucher-drivers.
- ❖ Ask departing guests whether they have made any charge purchases or place long distance telephone calls which do not appear on their folio.

While most guests will respond honestly to a direct question, many guests may not feel obligated to volunteer information about charges not posted to the folio. These guests will simply pay the outstanding balance on the folio and disregard un-posted charges. Guests are frequently unaware that they are responsible for paying un-posted charges.

Front office management at a non-automated or semi-automated property may establish a system to ensure that revenue outlet charges are delivered quickly to the front desk for posting especially during peak morning check-out periods. The front desk may employ runners to pick up revenue outlet vouchers, or may exchange voucher information by telephone. A pneumatic tube network may also be used to relay information between departments - similar to the way materials are relayed between clients and tellers at a drive- through bank.

A front office computer system that interfaces with revenue center outlets is often the most effective means of reducing or even eliminating late charges. A restaurant point-of-sale interface can instantly verify room account status, check credit authorization, and pot charges to the guest's folio - before the guest leaves the restaurant. Similarly, a call accounting system interface can help eliminate telephone late charges. Guests who make telephone calls from their guestroom and then go directly to the front desk to checkout will find all their telephone charges listed on their folio. Call accounting system interface will instantly post a telephone charge as soon as the call is completed.

Some front offices find that requiring a room key deposit at registration helps reduce unpaid account balances. Eager to retrieve their deposits, guests will more than likely return to the front desk before they leave the hotel. While refunding a deposit, the front office cashier has an opportunity to retrieve the guest's folio, search for any late charges, and complete the settlement process.

Guest who presents a credit card at check in time may assume that all charges will automatically be transferred to their credit card for billing. Depending on the agreement with the credit card company, the hotel may simply write "signature on file" on the signature of the credit card voucher and receive payment for the guest's outstanding balance. Some credit card companies allow after-departure charges to be added to the guest's credit card voucher. Front desk agent must be sure that this is permitted by hotel management and the credit card company before adding charges to a voucher the guest has

Sometimes guests do not mean to leave the hotel without paying. A guest may be in a hurry and actually forget to settle his or her account. In any case, the front office must be sure that the guest has left without paying before indicating so on the room status report. Such an error could be detrimental to effective rooms' management and to the hotel's guest

Collection of Accounts

Late charges that are billed to former guests should not be classified un-collectible until the front office has exhausted all billing and collection procedures. A properly completed registration card contains the guest's signature and his or her home and business addresses and telephone numbers. Procedures for billing late charges may be different for a guest who settled by cash than for a guest who settled by credit card. Guests who paid with a credit card will be billed according to the policies and procedures of the credit card company for late charge collection.

Guests' accounts not settled at check-out by cash payment in full - regardless of the credit established or prepayments made during registration - are transferred from the guest ledger to the city (non guest) ledger for collection. At that time, the guest account is transferred from the control of the front office to the accounting division.

Typical City Ledger Accounts Include:

- ❖ Credit card billings to authorized credit card companies.
- ❖ Direct billings to approved company and individual accounts.
- ❖ Travel agent accounts for authorized tours and groups.
- ❖ Bad check accounts resulting from former guests whose personal checks were returned unpaid.
- ❖ Skipper accounts for guests who left the hotel without paying the bill.
- ❖ Disputed bills for guests who refused to settle their accounts (in part or in full) based on a discrepancy.
- ❖ Guaranteed reservation accounts for billing no-show guests.
- ❖ Late charges accounts for guests who checked out before some charges were posted to their accounts.
- ❖ House accounts for non-guest business and promotional activities.
- ❖ To be successful, a hotel must establish a policy for billing former guests with overdue accounts. Typically, management determines the procedures and billing cycle appropriate for the hotel and its clientele. Deferred billing includes determining:
- ❖ When outstanding account balances are payable
- ❖ The number of days between billings
- ❖ How to control former guests whose accounts are overdue

The sooner the collection process is started, the sooner the hotel is likely to receive payment on deferred accounts. Timing is often the key to success in preparing former guest and non-guest accounts for collection. Each property uses its own collection schedule. Collection schedule can range from aggressive (short cycle) to lenient (long cycle) depending on the property's needs, clientele, profile, history of collection problems, and so on. Exhibit 9.3 shows a billing scheduling chart which may be used to develop or outline the methods and timing cycles for deferred payment - or account receivable - billings.

In all cases, it is important for staff to be polite - but firm - in any encounter involving a deferred payment account. Collection activities that violate a consumer's rights can be more costly than the original debt. The Federal Fair Debt Collection Practices Act and the Fair Credit billing Act clearly state the responsibilities and rights of those involved in.

Regardless of the collection procedures followed, problems in accounts receivable billing may develop. The hotel should have a procedure for collecting overdue accounts. Some hotels appoint a credit committee to examine overdue and decide among collection options.

Some properties attribute un-collectible accounts to the department which originally accepted the charge. Pro instance, the front office may be charged the amount of the uncollectible transaction if the post office returns a wrongly addressed billing. Postal returns can happen when a front desk agent does not ask the guest to clarify illegible writing on a registration card. Tracking receivable back to the originating departments may help identify departments whose procedures regularly result in un-collectible account balances. The credit committee, credit manager, or general manager can then analyze the departments' procedures - or lack of them - and take necessary corrective action. Collection problems may indicate the need for retraining employees or supervising them more closely.

Night Audit

The night audit is the daily review of guest account transactions against revenue center transactions, which help guarantee the accuracy of front office accounting system.

A successful audit will result in balanced guest and non-guest account, accurate account statements, appropriate account credit monitoring and timely reports to the management. An effective audit also increases the possibility or probability of correct account settlement Front office audit is usually called night audit because hotels generally perform it at night Before automated system became available the most convenient time to perform the audit was during the late evening and early morning hours.

Functions of Night Audit

The chief purpose of the night audit is to verify the accuracy and completeness of guest and non-guest accounts (non-guest accounts is also known as city account) against

Specifically The Night Audit is Concerned with The Following Functions:

1. Verify posted entries to guest and non-guest accounts.
2. Balancing all front office accounts.
3. Resolving room status discrepancies.
4. Producing operational and managerial reports.

Role of The Night Auditor

Performing the night audit requires attention to accounting details, procedural control and guest credit restrictions. The night auditor should also be familiar with the nature of cash transactions affecting the front office accounting systems. Night auditor typically tracks room revenue, occupancy percentage and other standard operating statistics. He or she also prepares a daily summary of the cash and credit card activities that took place at the front desk. These data reflect the front office's financial performance of the day. Night auditor summarizes and reports the result of the operations to the management.

Establishing An End of The Day

The night auditor generally works the night shift from 11 p.m. to 7 a.m. compiling, balancing and reviewing the transactions from the previous day. Each front office must decide what time will be considered the end of its accounting day, An end of day is simply an arbitrary stopping point for business activity. The front office must establish an end of the day so that the audit can be considered complete through a specific point in time. Usually the closing time of hotel revenue outlet determines the end of the day. In case of hotels with 24 hour room service, restaurants or stores the official end of the day is the time when the majority of the outlets close. Typically the business day ends when the night audit begins.

Cross Referencing

Hotel generates volumes of paper work and document transactions. For each revenue center transaction the originating revenue center document the transaction type (cash or paid out) and it's monitory value. Front office personnel post an entry to the appropriate guest or non-guest folio based on the documentation they receive.

A front office accounting system depends on transactional documentation to establish accurate records and maintain affective operational control. Transactional document identifies the nature and the amount of transaction and is the basis for data input in the front office accounting system. This documentation consists of guest checks and charge vouchers.

For internal control purpose an accounting system should provide independent supporting documentation to verify each transaction in non-automated or semi-automated operations. Supporting documents produced by different individuals provide cross-reference.

The night auditor relies on the transaction document to prove that proper accounting procedures were followed. The night auditor's review of daily posting reconciles front office accounts against revenue center and departmental records.

Accounts Integrity

Sound internal controls technques help ensure the accuracy completeness and integrity of front office accounting process. Proper internal control techniques suggests that different front office staff members post verify and collect for sale transactions at front desk.

The night auditor ensures that the hotel receives payments for goods and services. The night auditor establishes guest and non-guest account integrity by cross-referencing account posting with departmental source documentation. The audit process is complete when the total for guest, non-guest and departmental accounts are imbalanced or proven correct. As long as the audit process presents an out of balance position, the audit is considered incomplete. In essence an out of balance position exists when the charges and credits posted to the guest and non-guest accounts during the day do not match the charges and credits posted to the individual revenue sources. An out of balance condition may require a thorough review of all account statements, vouchers and departmental support documentation.

Guest Credit Monitoring

Supervising the credit limits of guest and non-guest account help maintain the integrity of front office accounting system. Establishing lines of credit limits depends on many factors such as credit card company flow limit, hotel house limits or guest status or reputation as a potential credit risk. The night auditor should be familiar with these limits and how to relate to each account. High account balances should be noted as part of the accounting process at the close of each business day the night auditor should identify the guest and non-guest accounts which have reached or exceeded their assigned credit limits. These accounts are typically called High Balance Accounts and the report generated is called High Balance Report.

Audit Posting Formula

Previous Balance + Debit - Credit = Net Outstanding Balance.

Daily And Supplement Transcript

A daily transcript is a detailed report of all guest account A daily transcript indicates those guest accounts that had transactional activity on that particular day. A supplement transcript is often used to record the day's transactional activities for non-guest account. Together the daily transcript and the supplement transcript detail all transactions occurring on a single day.

A daily transcript is typically detailed by revenue center, transaction type and transactional total. The detail transcript and supplement transcript from the basis for a consolidated report of front office accounting data against which departmental total can be.

Night audit procedures may be performed manually, mechanically or electronically. There are three modes in relation to night audit routine.

In a non-automated (manual) system, four forms are typically used to complete the audit. The system also uses transactional vouchers produced by the hotels revenue center and sent to the front desk. The four common night audit forms are:

(D) Audit Recapitulation Sheet.

The night auditor prepares daily and supplement transcript by copying the day's activity from each guest and non-guest account folio to the appropriate line on the transcript. The transcript columns are then summarized to determine the total charge transaction for each day. Information from these two transcripts along with the data from the cash sheet may be transferred to recapitulation sheet Few large front office operations rely on manual audit process.

1. Semi-Automated

One of the most important developments in the history of front office procedures has been the account-posting machine. Posting machine records guest charges on folios and simultaneously performs a number of other activities which simplify the work of the front desk agent and night auditor. Posting machines may be electro mechanical or electronic. The electronic systems are usually enhanced version of the old electro mechanical machines. Posting machines are only capable of producing a limited number of departmental totals, do not retail folio balance and do not interface with other systems (such as food and beverages point of sale system). Typically, front desk agent post charges to the account folio based on vouchers received from the hotels revenue outlet.

Forms produced in semi-automated audit system include a front office cash report and night auditor's summary report also called "D-Card".

2. Fully Automated

Of the three operating modes a fully automated audit process is by far the simplest and most reliable. Fully automated system can be interfaced with point of sale equipment, call accounting systems and other revenue center devices for quick accurate and automatic posting to electronic guest and non-guest account folios.

Night Audit Process

The discovery and collection of accounting error is what the night audit process is about. A night audit ensures the integrity of accounts through cross-referencing. Ledger accounts are compared to source documents from revenue center to prove individual entries and accounts total.

Discrepancies found during a might audit must be corrected. A night audit is conducted on a daily basis due to the transactional nature of the hotel business.

The degree of scrutiny required during the night audit process depends on the frequency of errors and volume of transactions to be checked. While the first of these factors related to the quality of front office work, the second co-relates with the size and complexity of the hotel. Large, complex hotels typically require closer accounts scrutiny

The Following Steps Are Common To The Sequence of Night Audit.

1. Complete Outstanding Posting

One of the primary functions of the night audit is to ensure that all transactions affecting guest and non-guest accounts are posted to appropriate folios before the end of the day. It is important to accurately post and account for all transactions on the day they occurred. Charges posted to the guest folio with the wrong dates will confuse guest. Generally guest will challenge such charges during checkout. This can cause delay for the guest and for the staff since the charges will have to be researched for an explanation.

Traditionally the first step of the night audit is to complete all outstanding postings. While sound front office practice dictates that transactions be posted to the proper accounts as they are received, the night auditor must confirm that all transactions have been posted before starting the audit routine. This actually means waiting until all food and beverages outlets, including the banquets facilities are closed. Incomplete posting will cause error in account balancing and complicate summary reporting.

In addition to completing the posting function the night auditor verifies that all vouchers for revenue center transactions are posted.

2. Reconcile Room Status Discrepancies

Room status discrepancies must be resolved in a timely manner since they can cause confusion in the front office. Errors in room status can lead to loss of room revenue. The front office must maintain current and accurate room status information to effectively determine the number and types of room available for sale. For example, if a guest checks out but the front desk agent fails to properly complete the checkout procedure the guest room may appear occupied when it is actually vacant. This could prevent the room from being rented until the error is discovered.

Before the end of the day the night auditor reconciles discrepancies between the daily housekeepers report and front office room status report.

To minimize errors housekeeping department typically requires the staff to record the perceived status of all rooms served. The auditor must review front office and housekeeping department reports to reconcile and finalized the occupancy status of all rooms for a given night.

If the housekeeping report indicates that a room is vacant, but the front office believes it is occupied, the auditor should search for an active room folio. If the folio exists and has an outstanding balance there are several possibilities:

- The guest may have departed but forgot to checkout.
- The guest may be a skipper who left with no intention of checking out.

- The front desk agent or cashier may not have properly closed the folio at checkout. After verifyi lg that the guest has left the hotel the night audit should process the checkout and set the folio aside for management review. If the folio has been settled the front office room status system should be corrected to show that the room is vacant. The night auditor should verify the guest folio against the housekeeping and the room status report to ensure that all three are

3. Balance All Departments

The night audit process can become quite complicated when errors are discovered. It is generally considered more efficient to balance all departments first and then look for individual posting errors within an out of balance department.

The night auditor balances all revenue center departments using source documents. The night auditor seeks to balance all front office accounts against departmental transactional information. Vouchers received at the front desk and other documents are totaled and compared to the revenue center summaries. Even fully automated hotels generally maintain source document because they can help resolve discrepancies should they arise.

4. Verify Room Rates

The night auditor may need to complete room revenue and account report. This report provides a means for analyzing room revenue since it shows the rack rate for each room and actual at which the room was sold. If the room rack and the actual rate do not match the night auditor should consider the following factors:

- If the room is occupied by a member of a group or a co-operate customer is it a discounted rate is offered?
- If there is only one guest in a room and the actual rate is approximately half the rack rate, is the guest part of the shared reservation? If he or she is, did a second guest registration.
- If the room is complementary, is the appropriate supporting back Up for the rate (for example, a complementary room authorized form).

5. Verify No Show Reservations

The night auditor may also be responsible for clearing the reservation rack and posting charges to no show accounts. In posting no show charges the night auditor must be careful to verify that the reservation was guaranteed and the guest never registered with the hotel. Sometimes duplicate reservations may be made for a guest. If these are not identified by the front office or the reservation employees, the guest may actually arrive but appear to be a no show under the second reservation. No show billing must be handled with great care. A front office that neglects to record cancellations properly and bills clients incorrectly risks having its legal agreement and relationship with the credit card companies re-evaluated. It may also risk losing the guests future business and the business of travel agency which

6. Post Room Rate and Taxes

Posting room rates and room taxes to all guest folios take place at the end of the day. Once room rate and taxes are posted, a room rate and a tax report may be generated for the front office manager. The ability to electronically is one of the most common advantages of automated system over manual and semi-automated system with manual or semi-automated system this can take hours.

7. Prepare Reports

The night auditor prepares reports which indicate status of front office activity. Among those prepared for management review are the final departmental details and summary report, the daily operational report, a high balance report and other report specific to the property.

- Final Departmental Detail and Summary report are produced and filed with the source documents for the accounting division. These reports help prove all transactions were properly accounted.

- The Daily Operational Report Summarizes the day's business and provides inside into revenue, receivables, operating statistics and cash transactions related to the front office.

- High Balance Report. Identifies guest approaching an account credit limit.

8. Deposit Cash

The night auditor frequently prepares a cash deposit voucher as part of the night audit process. If front office cash receipt have not yet been deposited. The night auditor compares the posting of cash payments and paid out with actual cash on hand. A copy of the cashier shift report may be included in the cash deposit envelope to support any overage, shortage or due back balances.

9. Clear or Backup The System

In manual and semi-automated hotels, totals must be cleared from the system after the entire night audit is complete. Manual systems are cleared by simply moving the closing balance from the night audit report to the opening balance of the next report In semi-automated hotels the total is the posting machine must be brought to zero. The night auditor controls this functioning so that the possibility of fraud is minimized.

Since a computer system eliminates the need for a room rack, reservation card and a variety of other traditional front office forms and devices, the front office depends on continuous functioning of the computer system. The back up step in the night audit routine is unique to computerize front office system. Backup reports must be run and various media duplicated in a timely manner so that the front office can run smoothly should the computer system fail.

End of day can be developed and automatically generate by a front office computer systems. Normally at least two guest lists are prepared for backup and emergency use; for the front desk and other for the telephone operator. A printed room status report enables front desk agent to identify vacant and ready rooms, should the.

Computer based information should be recorded (backup) on to a magnetic tape or disk, depending on system configuration. A system backup should be conducted after each night audit and stored in a safe place.

Many computer systems have two kinds of system back-ups. The daily backup creates copies of the systems electronic files on magnetic tape or disk in case of computer failure. The second type of system backup is performed once or twice a week. This backup not only backs up the daily information but eliminates account and transactions information no longer needed.

10. Distribute Reports

Due to the sensitive and confidential nature of front office information the night auditor must promptly deliver appropriate reports to the authorized individually.

Front Office Accounting System

A FO accounting system monitors and charts the transactions of guests and businesses, agencies and other non-guests using the hotel's services and facilities. An effective accounting system consists of tasks performed during each stage of the guest cycle. During the pre-arrival stage a guest accounting system captures data related to the type of reservation guarantee and tracks payments made earlier and advance deposits. When a guest arrives at the front desk, the guest accounting system documents the application of room rate and tax at registration. During occupancy, the accounting system tracks authorized guest purchases. Finally, a guest accounting system ensures payment for outstanding goods and services at the time of checkout.

In Brief, A FO Accounting System

- ✓ Creates And Maintains An Accurate Accounting Record For Each Guest or Non-Guest
- ✓ Tracks Financial Transactions Through The Guest Cycle n Ensures Internal Control Over Cash And Non-Cash Transactions
- ✓ Records Settlement For All Goods And Services Provided

The following accounting fundamentals are discussed below:

Accounts Folios Vouchers Points of Sale Ledgers

An Account is a form on which financial data are accumulated and summarized. It is a record of charges and payments. Adding a charge or payment is called posting to the account. A charge that is posted to a customer is called a debit, and a payment is called a credit. When a debit is posted, the amount of the debit is added to the account. When a credit is posted, the amount is subtracted. The increases and decreases in an account are calculated and the resulting monetary amount is the account balance. The value of debits and credits results from the use of double-entry book keeping, which is the basis for accounting in all modem businesses.

Guest Account

Guest account is a record of financial transactions, which occur between a guest and the hotel. Guest accounts are created when guests guarantee their reservations or when they register at the front desk. The FO usually seeks payment for any outstanding guest balance during the settlement stage of the guest cycle.

Non-Guest Account

A hotel may extend in-house charge privileges to local businesses or agencies as a means of promotion, or to groups sponsoring meetings at the hotel. The FO creates non-guest accounts to track these transactions, which may also be called house accounts or city accounts.

Folios

FO transactions are typically charted on account statements called folios. A folio is a statement of all transactions (debits and credits) affecting the balance of a single account. When an account is created, it is assigned a folio with a starting balance of zero. All debits and credits are recorded on the folio, and at settlement, a guest folio should be returned to zero balance by cash payment or by transfer to an approved credit card or direct billing account.

There are basically five types of folios used in FO accounting:

1. Guest Folios: accounts assigned to individual persons or guest rooms

2. Master Folios: accounts assigned to more than one person or guest room, usually applicable for group accounts.

3. Non-Guest or Semi-Permanent Folios: accounts assigned to non-guest business or agencies with hotel charge purchase privileges.

4. Employee Folios: accounts assigned to employees with charge purchase

5. Split Folios: accounts assigned to a guest on his/her request to split his/her charges and payments between two personal folios - one to record expenses to be paid by the sponsoring business company, and the other to record personal expenses to be paid by the guest. In this case, two folios are created for the same

A voucher details a transaction to be posted to a FO account. This document lists detailed transaction information gathered at the source of the transaction. The voucher is then sent to the FO for posting. Several types of vouchers are used in FO accounting such as, cash vouchers, charge vouchers, transfer vouchers, allowance vouchers, paid-out vouchers.

1. Cash Voucher is a voucher used to support a cash payment transaction at the front desk.

2. Charge Voucher is a voucher used to support a charge purchase transaction that takes place somewhere other than the front desk, and also referred to as an account receivable voucher.

3. Allowance Voucher is a voucher used to support an account allowance.

4. Cash Advance Voucher is a voucher used to support cash flow out of the hotel, either directly to or on behalf of a guest.

5. Correction Voucher is a voucher used to support the correction of a posting error which is rectified before the close of business on the day the error was made.

6. Credit Card Voucher is the form designated by a credit card company to be used for imprinting a credit card and recording the amount charged.

7. Paid - out Voucher is a voucher used to support the cash disbursed by the hotel on behalf of a guest and charged to the guest's account as a cash advance.

8. Transfer Voucher is a voucher used to support a reduction in balance on one folio and an equal increase in balance on another. Transfer vouchers are used for transfers between guest accounts and for transfers from guest accounts to non-guest accounts when they are settled by the use of credit cards.

9. Travel Agency Voucher is a type of travel agent guaranteed reservation in which the agent forwards a voucher to the hotel as proof of payment and guarantees that the prepaid amount will be sent the hotel when the voucher is returned to the travel agency for payment.

Points of Sale (Pos)

The term point of sale describes the location at which goods or services are purchased. Any hotel department that collects revenues for its goods and services is considered a revenue centre, and thus, a point of sale. The FO accounting system must ensure that all charge purchases at these points of safe are posted to the proper guest or non-guest account. A computerized POS system may allow remote terminals at the points of sale to communicate directly with a FO computer system, and helps FO staff to create a well- documented, legible folio statement with a minimum number of errors. Some basic information, which must be provided by a POS, includes the amount of the charge, name of the POS outlet, room number and name of the guest, and brief description of the charge.

A ledger is a summary grouping of accounts. A FO ledger is a collection of FO account folios. The folios represented in the FO are a part of the FO accounts receivable ledger. An accounts receivable represents money owed to the hotel. FO accounting uses two ledgers :

Guest Ledger: refers to the set of guest accounts that correspond to registered hotel guests. Guests financial transactions are recorded onto guest ledger accounts to assist in tracking guest account balances. The guest ledger is also known as Transient ledger, or Front Office Ledger or Rooms Ledger.

City Ledger: also called the non-guest ledger, is the collection of non-guest accounts. If a guest account is not settled in full by cash payment at checkout, the guest's folio balance is transferred from the guest, ledger in the FO to the city ledger in the accounting division for collection. The city ledger can contain credit card payment accounts, direct billing accounts, and accounts of past guests due for collection by the hotel.

Creation And Maintenance of Accounts

Guest folios are created during the reservations process or at the time of registration. To prepare a folio for use, information from the guest's reservation or registration record must be transferred to the folio. Non-automated and semi-automated systems commonly use pre-numbered folios for internal control purposes, and the folio number is usually entered onto the GRC for cross-referencing. Manually posted or machine-posted guest folio cards arc stored in a front desk folio tray, which is also referred to as a folio well or bucket. In a computerized system, guest information is automatically transferred from an electronic reservation or registration record and entered onto an electronic folio, which is crossreferenced automatically with other computer-based records within the FO system. In some systems, a preliminary electronic folio is created automatically and simultaneously with the reservation record.

Accounting Systems

Non-Automated; Guest folios in a manual system contain a series of columns for listing debit and credit entries accumulated during occupancy. At the end of the business day, each column is totaled and the ending balance (closing balance) is carried forward as the opening balance of the following day.

Semi-Automated : Guest transactions are printed sequentially on a machine-posted folio with information including date, department / reference number, amount of the transaction, and new balance of the account. A column labeled "previous balance pick-up" provides an audit trail within the posting machine framework that helps prove the current

Fully Automated: POS transactions may. be automatically posted to an electronic folio. When a printed copy of a folio is needed, debits and credits may appear in a single column with payments distinguished by parentheses, i.e. ( ) or a minus sign -. Computer-based systems maintain current balances for all folios.

Credit Monitoring

The FO must monitor guest and non-guest accounts to ensure that they remain within acceptable credit limits. Guests who present an acceptable credit card at registration may be extended credit facility equal to the floor limit authorized by the issuing credit card company. Guest and non-guest accounts with other approved credit arrangements are subject to limitations established by the FO, called House Limits. The FO auditor or Night Auditor is primarily responsible for identifying accounts, which have reached or exceeded predetermined credit limits. Such accounts are called high-risk or high balance accounts. The FO may deny additional charge purchase privileges to guests with high balance accounts until the situation is resolved through requesting the guest to make a partial payment or requesting the credit card company to authorize additional credit.

Front Office Accounting Formula

Transaction postings in the FO conform to a basic FO accounting formula, which is : Previous Balance + Debits - Credits = Net Outstanding Balance PB + Dr. - Cr. = NOB

Internal Control in The Front Office
Internal Control in The FO Involves:

i. Tracking transaction documentation

ii. Verifying account entries and balances

iii. Identifying vulnerabilities in the accounting system

Auditing is the process of verifying FO accounting records for accuracy and completeness. Each financial interaction produces, paperwork which documents the nature and amount of the transaction, and these documents should be checked to ensure that proper postings have been made to the correct accounts. Certain instruments are used to exercise control in FO Cash, as described below:

Front Office Cash Sheet: The FO is responsible for a variety of cash transactions affecting both guest and non-guest accounts, and FO cashiers may be required to complete a FO Cash Sheet that lists each receipt or disbursement of cash. The information contained on a FO Cash Sheet is used to reconcile cash on hand at the end of a cashier shift with the documented transactions which occurred during the shift.

Cash Bank: A second set of FO accounting control procedures involves the use of FO cashier banks. A cash bank is an amount of cash assigned to a cashier so that he/she can handle the various transactions that occur during a particular work shift. Cashiers should sign for their bank at the beginning of their shift, and only the person who signs for the bank should have access to it. At the end of a shift, each cashier is solely responsible for depositing all cash, checks and other negotiable instruments received during the shift. The cashier separates out the amount of the initial bank, and then places the remaining cash, checks, etc. in a specially designed cash voucher or FO cash envelope. The cashier normally itemizes and records the contents of the envelope on its outside before depositing it into the FO vault, which should be witnessed by another employee, and both employees should sign a log attesting the deposit was actually done, and stating the time of the deposit.

Net Cash Receipts = Amount of Cash, Checks, Vouchers, etc. in the

Amount of initial Cash Bank + Paid Outs

Averages (i.e. total of cash and checks in a cash drawer is greater than the initial cash bank + net cash receipts) or Shortages (i.e. total of cash and checks in cash drawer is less than the initial cash bank + receipts) are determined by comparing the cash totals of the cashier's postings against the actual cash, checks and negotiable instruments in the cashier's bank.

Due Back: A due back occurs when a cashier pays out more than he / she receives,

ie. in other words, there is not enough cash in the drawer to restore the initial cash bank. Such a situation may arise when a cashier accepts many checks and large bills, or encashes large amount of foreign exchange offered by guests during a shift, whereby, a large amount of outflow of cash from the bank takes place. These checks and bills are deposited with other receipts, and consequently, the FO deposit may be greater than the cashier's net cash receipts, with the excess "due back" to the FO cashier's bank. FO due backs are normally replaced with small bills (notes) and coins before the cashier's next shift, thereby restoring the cash bank to its full and correct amount.

Audit Control: Apart from the above mentioned measures to verify correct proceedings in the FO cash, internal auditors may make unannounced visits to the cashier's desk for the purpose of auditing accounting records, as well as conducting spot-checks of the cash bank of the cashier on duty. A report is duly completed for management and

Settlement of Accounts

The collection of payment for outstanding account balances is called account settlement, which involves bringing an account balance to zero. An account can be brought to a zero balance as a result of a cash payment in full or a transfer to an approved direct billing or credit card account. All guest accounts must be settled at the time of check-out. Transfers to approved deferred payment plans move outstanding guest folio balances from

Handling Situations

D. N. S (Did Not Stay)

The guest sometimes wants to move out almost immediately being shown into his room. If the room is not satisfactory to the guest, the receptionist must try to provide alternative accommodation (even in another hotel). If the guest departs for reason that are beyond the hotel's control, the receptionist should express his regrets of assists the guest in departure. If the room has not been used, no charge will be made to the guest. All forms and records should be marked "DNS". The management normally wants to be informed about all the DNS cases.

N.A (Did Not Arrive)

At the end of the day, the cleric or receptionist should take the following steps:

1. If there is reservation slip in the Reservation Rack.
2. Check the room information rack that the guest did not check in already.
3. Check with the airlines, if the airline numbers are given.
4. Attach the time-stamped reservation to the folio and mark DNA if guaranteed or
5. No DNA or reservation form and place it with next days arrival often a guest

R.N A (Registered But Not Assigned)

A guest arriving early in the morning when rooms are not available may be as to register, deposit luggage with the bell desk and return to the hotel for the room assignment later in the day. The registration card is kept at the desk with the notation RNA. As soon as the room will be available the assignment is made. This is possible with traveling executives.

Paid in Advance (No Luggage)

If the guest does not have luggage, payment is advance is normally requested. This situation should be handled with extreme care and tact. If the guest holds a credit card, an imprint can be made and an advance payment need not be requested.

If it is the policy of the hotel to collect the room rate in advance in "No Luggage" cases the reception should inform the guest politely and carefully collect the amount for one night accommodation gave a receipt and treat the guest politely.

After the check in the Front Office, cashier and sales outlets will be informed that the guest should pay in cash.

No Information

The guest may request that no information regarding their presence in this hotel be given to the calls. The "No Information" should be clearly marked on the slips so that the staff can respond appropriately.

Pre-Registration

To avoid unnecessary delay in checking a pre-registration system is used in many hotels for frequent guest, business travellers and groups. The following can be carried out if the :

1. The rooms are blocked on the room rack.
2. Registration forms are typed out, Guest need only to sign on arrival.
3. Guest folio (bills) is opened for group and for individuals.
4. Rack slips are typed out (this is done only if the customer is confirmed).
5. A separate counter is used to check in the groups.
6. The group leader obtains the signature of group members on registration card and
7. Each guest receives an envelope containing key, welcome card, chart instructions, tour or convention information, tourist information too.
8. The bellman will move the guest to the room and take care of the luggage.

As a policy, all the hotels overbook to a certain percentage. The percentage of overbooking is normally determined by past experience. This is to obtain high occupancy percentage even there are "No-Show" cancellation at the last minute (No-show is a customer or guest who has a confirmed reservation but does not turn up).

Forecasting may be affected by certain factors:

1. More cancellations than anticipated.
2. People wanting to check in without a prior reservation (walk-in).
3. More no shows than anticipated.
4. Guests who overstay.
5. Rooms taken under repairs.
6. Faulty over-bookings.
7. Addition or reduction of the guest rooms that affect the number of saleable rooms.

Sold Out

These are rooms over-booked (full house).

Free Sale

It's a day when rooms are available.

Vip And Special Attention Guest And Distinguished Attention Guest (Spatt)

This is normally noted at the reservation forms to alert the front office and the reservation staff and housekeeping to give the person special attention. SPATT are often assisted by front office manager or lobby manager and accompanied to the room. The VIP represents either good publicity to the hotel or direct business. Examples : Company President, Conference Organizers and Royal Guest. Distinguished guests are honored for his position rather than his econom al value rather than money, example, Royal Guest Dignitaries.

Managing Hospitality

The concept of hospitality, the generous and cordial provision of services to a guest, is at the heart of our industry. These services, in the hotel industry, can include room accommodations, food, and beverages, meeting facilities reservations, information on hotel services, information on local attractions, etc. guests who feel they are not treated with respect or have not received full value of their dollar will seek out others who they believe do provide hospitality. As you prepare for a career in an industry that may differentiate its product by continual and efficient delivery of professional hospitality service, these basic rudiments will serve as a primer for your development.

Definition of Hospitality

Hospitality means the whole process of anticipating and satisfying a guest's needs. This goes right back to the design stage and covers facilities and staffing levels in relation to what the would-be guest is willing to pay

Importance of Hospitality

Hospitality is a very important consideration for both guest and the hotel entrepreneur. Every guest expects and deserves hospitable treatment. Providing hospitality to meet guest need involves not only a positive attitude, but an array of services that make the guest's stay

The success or Mure in providing hospitality often determines the success or failure of the hotel. Capitalizing on opportunities to provide hospitality is essential. What do these issues & delivering hospitality to the guest mean to the entrepreneur? They emphatically imply that the guest who is not treated with hospitality will choose to do business with the competitor and may also influence others not to try your hotel for the first time or not to continue to do business with you. The entrepreneur who is aware of the competition realizes that this negative advertising will severely affect the profit-and-loss statement.

If a hotel does not provide the desired level of service to ten guests on any given day, only one guest will bring the complaint to the attention of the hotel staff. If the complaint is resolved quickly, this one person will almost surely do business again with the hotel. On the other hand, the nine guests who did not bring their complaints to the attention of the hotel staff will probably not do business with the hotel again and each of them may tell approximately 20 people - 180 people will hear their negative account of the hotel.

The hotel never hears from 96% of its unhappy customers. For every complaint received the hotel in fact has 26 customers with problems, 6 of which are serious problems. Complainers are more likely to do business again with the hotel than non-complainers even if the problem isn't resolved satisfactorily. Customers who have complained to a hotel and their complaints satisfactorily resolved tell an average of five people about the treatment they received.

Delivering hospitality imply that the guest who is not treated with hospitality will choose to do business with a competitor and may also influence others not to try your hotel for the first time or not to continue to do business with you. The entrepreneur who is aware of the competition realizes that this negative advertising will severely affect the profit & loss statement.

The financial ramifications of so many people negatively impressed with your hotel are clearly disastrous. Hospitable treatment of guests must be more that just an option; it must be standard operating procedure. It is a concept that must be adopted as a corporate trend and organized for effective delivery.

Guest Needs

Quality is a function of the extent to which the hotel satisfies the full range of guest needs, taking price info consideration. It is necessarily a subjective assessment on the part of the individual guest, but if we could somehow combine the various elements we should be able to arrive at an aggregate quality rating in respect of any hotel. A possible mechanism for determining this might be as follows :

- $F =$ Range of facilities or amenities (eg. Bath, TV, pool etc.)
- $C =$ Standard of comfort (eg. Warmth, quietness, cleanliness etc.)
- $A =$ Ambience (eg. Attractiveness of decor etc.)
- $R =$ Range of services available (eg. Parking, concierge, room service etc.)
- $S =$ Speed or promptness of staff service
- $H =$ Hospitality (eg. Warmth of the staffs welcome)
- $P =$ Price (eg. High, average or low)

The idea is to give a score for each of the package elements. This might be as simple as 3 to 1, with 3 meaning above expectations and the opposite. Price would be scored on a broadly similar basis with 3 meaning higher than expected and 1 that it is perceived to be low. This quality rating is only intended as a conceptual structure about quality in relation to the hotel package.

Managing The Delivery of Hospitality

It is not enough for the FOM to decide that the members of the Front Office should provide good service and display hospitality to guests. To provide satisfactory hospitality to all guests at all times, FOM must develop and administer a service management program, which highlights a company's focus on meeting customer's needs and allows a hotel to achieve its financial goals. This program must be based on sound management principles, and the hotel's commitment to meeting those needs.

Management's Role

Management may decide to implement one or two specific; Management may feel the negative impact of the rude, lazy, or careless employee has caused unnecessary bad public relations. If a group of employees is not performing to management's standards, the cumulative effects of a group will take a toll in the long run. A comprehensive program aimed at meeting the needs of a hotel's prime market—guest, who continue to do business with the hotel—provides the foundation for long-term successful delivery of hospitality.

Service management is the most visible responsibility because it affects all the other objectives of the hotel. Often the people in staff positions in hotels become so involved with their day-to-day paper shuffling and deadlines that they forget why they are in business. The may not necessarily mean to forget, but it happens all too often. Service management ensures that there is a commitment to a long-range effort by appointing someone within the organization responsibility for developing, organizing, and delivering it.

The front office manager usually supervises service management efforts. Other key department heads, such as the food and beverage manager and director of marketing and sales, who supervise employees who deals with guests, rely on the organizational leadership of the front of the front office manager. It is important to note that the responsibility of delivering hospitality to the guest in each department is always a part of the job of each supervisor or shift leader, the person responsible for directing the efforts of a particular work shift. The organizational efforts provided by the front office manager serve as the basis for a homogeneous plan for the hotel.

The owner and general manager must make a financial commitment to ensure the success of the program. An important component of the program is motivating employees to deliver hospitality on a continual basis through incentive programs. Incentive programs are management's organized efforts to determine employees meet their needs and the need of hotel. Such programs reward the employee for providing constant and satisfactory guest service and often involve money in the form of bonuses, which must be budgeted in the annual projected budget.

The Service Strategy Statement

To produce an effective service management program, management must devise a service strategy statement, a formal recognition by management that the hotel will strive to deliver the products and services desired by the guest in a professional manner. To accomplish this, management must first identify the guest's needs.

Market Research, internal guest comments and regular employee attitude surveys all confirm that what has set and will continue to set the hotel apart from the competitors is the personal service. In addition to identifying generally what he guest want, management should survey guests about their hotel to determine what services they expect and how they want these services delivered. The GM may assign this task to the marketing & sales director, who may start reviewing and summarizing customer comment cards. A review of the ureas in which the hotel has disappointed its guests, will provide a basis for determining where to begin a guest survey. The problem areas identified from this study are then used as the focus of a simple survey form.

Guests want quick and efficient service. They want to avoid long lines. They want to find their way around the hotel and the immediate vicinity. They want the product and services in the hotel to work. If you use these observations as a baseline for beginning to understand guests needs while the yare away from home, you will be able to better satisfy their need.

Senior management cannot adequately determine what is desired at the customer level until a comprehensive evaluation of customer preference is established through a systematic consumer research study. Thus, in addition to identifying generally, what guests want; management should survey guests about their particular property to determine what services they expect and how they want these services delivered.

Cadotte and Turgeon have analyzed a survey concerning the frequency and types of complaints and compliments received by guests of members of the National Restaurant Association and the American Hotel & Motel Association:

1. **Dissatisfiers-** complaints for low performance, e.g., parking.

2. **Satisfier-** unusual performance apparently elicits compliments, but average performance or even the absence of the future Will probably not cause dissatisfaction or complaints, e.g.,

3. **Critical Variables-** capable of eliciting both positive and negative feelings, depending on the situation, e.g., cleanliness, quality of service, employee knowledge and service, and quietness of.

4. **Neutrals-** factors that received neither a great number of compliments nor many complaints are probably either not salient to guests or easily brought up to guest standards.

Albrecht and Zemke also identify general guest expectations as follows:
- Care and concern from service provider
- Spontaneity - people are authorized to think
- Problem solving - people can work out the intricacies of problems
- Recovery - will anybody make special efforts to set a problem right

Their conclusions add another dimension to the service strategy statement. In addition to certain recognizable products and services delivered at a certain speed and level of quality, guests expect employee to accept the responsibility for resolving problems. The guest should not encounter unconcerned staff or be bounced from employee to employee in order to have a problem solved. Management must develop a staff that can think and solve problems.

Developing Service Strategy Statement

After Management has identified what guests want, they can develop a SSS. The SSS should include:

i. A commitment from top-level management that service to make a top priority in the hotel.

ii. A commitment to develop and to administer a Service Management program

iii. A commitment to train employees to deliver service efficiently.

iv. A commitment of financial resources to develop incentives for the employees who deliver the services.

These directives will serve as guidelines in the development of a service management program. More important, they force management to think of service as a long-term effort and not as temporary solution.

Hotel managers who fail to develop a clear SSS and make a financial commitment to delivering hospitality experience find it extremely difficult in applying the principles of TQM. TQM requires an immense commitment of labour to analyze guest and employee interaction, reallocation of responsibilities and authority to foster an improvement in services and long-term commitment for learning a new method of management.

After a guest has requested for a product or service, a front office team develops a flow-chart, an analysis of the delivery of a particular product or service. Analysis of this interaction by the group of people who deliver the product or service allows for suggestions for improvement. A key component of TQM is the commitment for continuous analysis of delivery of guest services and plans for improvement.

Developing A Service Management Program

Employee involvement in planning a service management program is as important as obtaining a financial commitment from owners in establishing such a program. Too often, when the employees are not includes in the planning stages, they look at plan and remark, "This is ridiculous, not for me; let the people in marketing and sales worry about It." In many cases, service is perceived as just another fancy concept proposed by management Management needs to address that attitude from the onset. By getting employees involved early, they are much more likely to buy into the program, since they are already a part of it.

Guest Cycle

The FOM responsible for developing an effective SMP, along with other departmental heads, should first take a look at the employees they supervise. Representatives from all job categories and various shifts should be included on the planning committee, so that an effective program is developed. It allows the plans to be altered in the planning stages by those who must implement it and ensures clear, workable operational methods. It gives the employees time to adjust to the new concept while allowing time to develop adoption procedures. At each planning phase, employees learn how they will benefit from the program. This is a realistic approach to focus management's efforts in adopting this important concept.

Once the members of the planning committee have been chosen, the next step is to analyze the guest's perception of the hospitality system. The figure 1 illustrates the cycle of service, the progression of a guest's request for products and services through the departments of a hotel. This outline is presented only as a working tool for FOM to use in analyzing the hotel services the guest will encounter. In developing a list for a specific hotel, the employee input will be very useful

Another benefit of analyzing the cycle of service is that it may highlight inefficiencies built into the system. Rectifying these inefficiencies will assist in delivering first class hospitality.

Fig 1: Review of the cycle of services

Marketing

- Customer surveys before & after stay)
- Advertising: billboards, direct mail, radio, TV, print, internet, incentive promotions
- Toll-free numbers, fax, internet, CRS
- Telephone manners of reservationists

- Cancellation policy (reasonable restrictions)
- Accommodation availability (value and cost considerations)
- Complimentary services/products (value and cost considerations)
- Information on hotel shuttle and public transportation
- Hotel shuttle and public transportation
- Greetings (doorman, bell staff, front desk staff)
- Check-in procedure- length of time in line, ease of check in (preprinted GRC or self-registration)
- Room accommodations (value and cost considerations)
- Credit Card acceptance
- Complimentary services / products (value and cost considerations)
- Room Status / availability
- Information on other hotel services
- Clearness and interior design of lobby, elevators, room
- Amenities available

Guest Stay

Other Hotel Departments

- Food service departments
- (menu offerings, hours of operation, prices, service level, ambience)
- Gift shop (selection, souvenirs, value/price)
- Lounge (prices, entertainment, hours, service level)
- Room Service (menu offerings, prices, hours of availability, promptness in delivery
- and clearance)
- Valet service (pickup and delivery times, prices, quality of service)
- HK services (daily room cleaning, replenishment of amenities, cleanliness of public areas, requests for directions in hotel)
- Security (24-hour availability, fire safety devices, key and lock repair service,
- requests for directions in hotel)
- Front Office
- Requests for information and assistance (wake-up calls, hours of operation of other depts., transmits requests to other depts.)
- Reasonable and flexible checkout time deadlines

- Length of time in line
- Immediate availability of guest folio printout; accuracy of charges
- Additional reservations

Moments of Truth in Hotel Service Management

Every time the hotel guest comes in contact with some aspect of the hotel, he or she judges its hospitality. Guests who are told by a preservationist that they must "take this room a this rate or stay elsewhere" will not feel the hospitality is a primary consideration at this hotel. When a potential guest calls and asks to speak with Mr. General Manager and the switchboard operator answer, "Who is that?" that gust will expect the same kind of careless, impersonal treatment when (or it) he or she decides o say at that hotel. The guest who is crammed into an elevator with half the housekeeping crew, their vacuum cleaners, and bins soiled laundry will not feel welcomed. All these impressions make the guest feel that service at this hotel is mismanaged.

These examples are only some of the moments of truth that can be identified from an analysis of the guest service cycle. Albrecht and Zemke tell us that each guest has a "report card" in his or her head which s the basis of a grading system that leads the customer to decide whether to partake of the service again or to go elsewhere. This challenge is not to be viewed as mission impossible, but rather as an organized and concerted effort by owners, management, and employees.

Employee Buy-in Concept

All the sophisticated marketing programs, well-orchestrated sales promotions, outstanding architectural designs, degreed and certified management staff form only the backdrop for the delivery of hospitality. The front-line employee is "the" link in the service management program. He or she must deliver the service. It is simple fact that still amazes many people. How can front office managers ensure that front-line employees deliver a consistently high level of service?

Albrecht And Zemke Offer The Following Suggestions:

To have a high standard of service, it is necessary to create and maintain a motivating environment in which service people can find personal reasons for committing their energies to the benefit of the customer.

In short, only employees who are committed to the service management program will provide a consistently high level of service. Management fosters this commitment.

Consider employees in each hotel and determine how to stimulate their commitment to service. If money will motivate them, financial incentive programs that reward positive expressions of hospitality are in order. Employee stock ownership programs also provide an incentive for employees to realize financially the importance of delivering a consistently high level of hospitality. Other reward systems may include preferential treatment in scheduling shifts, longer vacations, and extra holidays. Long-range rewards may include

Screening Employees Who Deliver Hospitality

Anchor factor to consider in developing a service management program is the employee character traits needed to provide hospitality. When evaluating candidates for front-line service positions, interviews should be structured to screen out employees who are not able or willing to deal with the demands of guest service. Albreht and Zemke offer these considerations for choosing front-line employees: "a service person needs to have at least an adequate level of maturity and self esteem. He or she needs to be reasonably articulate, aware of the normal rules of social context, and be able to say and do what is necessary to establish rapport with a customer and maintain it. Third, he or she needs to have a high level of tolerance for contact.

Group discussion among the managerial staff will help to highlight the attributes of a person who will be able to deliver hospitality. These discussions should lead to a rather informal procedure for screening employees. Questions that determine whether candidates display maturity and self-esteem is articulate, possess social graces and have a high level of tolerance for continued guest contact can be discussed in-group settings. Managers who are aware of what they are looking for in employees are better able to secure the right people for the right jobs.

Training For Hospitality Management

Part of a service management programs involves employee training to deliver hospitality. Just as managers discuss what they want in an employee, managers decide what must be done to convey hospitality to travellers who are away from home.

The key to making training pay off is knowing what we want the trainees to be able to do when they have finished the program. An effective training process starts with a performance analysis. We must analyze the various jobs to be done in serving the customer well, and then spell out the knowledge, attitudes, and skills required of the person doing the job. The communications of hospitality must be identified, so that each employee can be trained to convey them.

Evaluating The Service Management Program

Any program requires methods for evaluating whether the program has successfully

Albrecht and Zemke base the development of sound evaluation procedure on identifying the guest's moments of truth. The more research put into identifying the components of the guest service cycle for a specific hotel property, the more effective managers and employees will be in evaluating service delivery. Specific desired behaviors could be identified and measured. Customer comment cards provide one of the ways hotel management and staff can receive feedback.

One other method that can be used to obtain useful feedback is by having front-line staff, such as a desk clerk; inquire about the guest's visit during checkout. A method of communicating gust responses to the appropriate departments, which can rectify the errors or reward the front-line employee, will complete the process of evaluating the success of a service management program.

All feedback must be communicated to the front-line employee for continuous improvement of service.

Follow Through

Vital to any service management program is the continued implementation of the program over time. Management can begin a service management program with the best of intensions, but too often, it is dropped or neglected in the day-to-day flurry of operations. The difference between a program and continuous commitment is management Management is the key to implementing an effective guest service program. The commitment to hospitality is not a casual one; it requires constant attention, research, training, and evaluation. Only with this commitment can a hotel ensure hospitality every day for every guest.

Planning And Evaluating Operations

Management Functions

The process of front office management can be divided into specific management functions.

Planning

Planning is probably the most important management function performed in any business. Without the direction and focus planning provides, the front office manager may become overly involved with tasks that are unrelated to or inconsistent with accomplishing the department's goal. A front office manager's first step in planning what the front office will accomplish is to define the department's goal. The front office manager should use these general goals as a guide to planning more specific, measurable objectives. Planning also includes determining the strategies that will be used to attain the objectives.

Using the planned goals as a guide, a front office manager organizes the department by dividing the work among front office staff. Work should be distributed so that everyone gets a fair assignment and all work can be completed in a timely manner. Organizing includes determining the order in which tasks are to be performed and establishing completion

Coordinating involves bringing together and using the available resources to attain planned goals. A front office manager must be able to coordinate the efforts of many individuals to ensure that the work is performed efficiently, effectively, and on time. A manager's ability t coordinate is closely related to his or her other management skills, such as planning and organizing.

Staffing

Staffing involves recruiting applicants and selecting those best qualified for positions. Staffing also involves scheduling employees'. Most front office managers develop staffing guidelines. These guidelines are usually based on formulas for calculating the number of employees required to meet guest and operational needs under specified conditions.

Leading

Leading is a complicated management skill that is exercised in a wide variety of situations, and is closely related t other management skills such as organizing, coordinating, and staffing. For a front office manager, leadership involves overseeing, motivating, training, disciplining, and setting an example for the front office staff. If the department is behind in getting the work done, the front office manager steps into the situation and assists until (he workload is under control again.

Controlling

Every front office has a system of internal controls for protecting the assets of the hotel. However, internal control systems work only when managers believe in the systems' importance and follow the established procedures for their use. The control process ensures that the actual results of operations closely match planned results.

Evaluating

Evaluating determines the extent to which panned goals are, in fact, attained. This task is frequently overlooked in many front office operations, or is performed haphazardly. Evaluating also involves reviewing and, when necessary, revising or helping to revise front office goals.

Three important front office planning function:

- Establishing room rates.

- Forecasting room availability.

- Budget for operations.

A front office will almost always have more than one room ate category for each of its guestrooms. Room rate categories generally correspond t types of rooms that are comparable in squire footage and furnishings. Differences are based on criteria such as room size, location, view, and furnishings. Each room rate category is assigned a rack rate based on the number of persons occupying the room. The rack rate is the standard price determined by front office management The rack rate is listed on the room rate schedule to inform front desk agents of the selling price each guest room in the hotel.

Front office employees are expected to sell rooms at the rack rate unless a guest qualifies for an alternate room rate. Special rates are often quoted to groups and certain guests for promotional purposes during low occupancy periods. Special room rate

- Corporate or commercial rate. The rate offered to companies that provide frequent business for the hotel or its chain.

- Group rate. The rate offered to groups, meetings, and conventions using hotel for their functions.

- Promotional rate. The rate offered to individual who may belong to an affinity group such as American Automobile Association or American Association of retired Persons to promote their patronage. The rate may also be extended during special low occupancy periods to any gust to promote occupancy.

- Incentive rate. The rate offered to guests in affiliated organizations such as travel agencies and airlines because of potential referral business. The rate may also be offered to promote future business; it is often extended to group leaders, meeting planners, tour operators, and other capable of providing the hotel with additional room sales.

- Family rate. A rate reserved for family with children.

- Package plan rate. A rate includes a guestroom in combination with other events or activities.

- Complimentary rate. A room rate provided to special guests and / or important industry leaders.

The front office manager must be sure that the sale of rooms at special rates in rigidly controlled. Special rates represent discounts from the rack rate and therefore may adversely affect the average room rate and room revenue.

Establishing rack rates for room type and determining discount categories and special rates are major management decisions. To establish room rates that will ensure the hotel's

Profitable, management should carefully consider such factors as operating costs, inflationary factors, and competition.

Room rates often serve as a market positioning statement since they directly reflect service expectations to the hotel's target a market. Room rate positioning can be critical to a hotel's success.

Market Condition Approach

This approach is the commonsense approach. Management looks at comparable hotels in the geographical market and sees what they are charging for the same product. The thought behind this is that the hotel can charge only what the market will accept, and this is

There are many problems with this approach, although it is used very often. First, if the property is new, construction costs will most likely be higher than those of the competition. Therefore, the hotel cannot be as profitable as the competition initially. Second, this approach does not take the value of the property into consideration. With the property being new, and perhaps having newer amenities, the value of the property to guests can be greater. The market condition approach is really a marketing approach that allows the local market to determine the rate.

Rule-of-Thumb Approach

The rule-of-thumb approach sets the rate of a room at Rs. 1 for each Rs. *1*000 of construction and furnishing cost per room, assuming 70% occupancy.

The emphasis placed on the hotel's construction cost fails to consider the effects of inflation. The Rule-of-Thumb approach to pricing rooms also fails to consider the contribution other facilities and services toward the hotels desired profitably. In man hotels, guests pay for service such as food, beverages, telephones, and laundry. If these services contribute to profitability, the hotel may have less pressure to charge higher room rates.

The rule-of-thumb approach should also consider the occupancy level of the hotel. Hotels tend to have a very high level of fixed expenses. For example, a mortgage payment is the same every stand the effects of room rate and room occupancy on room revenue to ensure that the hotel meets its revenue goals and financial obligations.

Hubbart Formula Approach

1. To determine the average selling price per room, this approach considers operating costs, desired profits, and expected number of rooms sold In the other words, these approach starts with desired profit, add income taxes, then adds fixed charges and management fees, followed by operating overhead expenses and direct operating expenses. The Hubbart

Formula is considered a bottom-up approach to pricing rooms because its initial item- net income (profit) - appears at the bottom of the income statement.

2. Calculate the hotel's desired profit by multiplying the desired rate of return (ROI) by the owners' investment.

3. Calculate pretax profits by dividing desired profits by 1 minus the hotel's tax rate.

4. Calculate the fixed charges and management fees. This calculation includes estimating depreciation, interest expense, property taxes, insurance, amortization, building mortgage, land, rent, and management fees.

5. Calculate undistributed operating expenses, this calculation includes estimating administrative and general, data processing, human resources, transportation, marketing, property operation and maintenance, and energy costs.

6. Estimate non-room operated department income or loss, that is, food and beverage department income or loss, telephone department income or loss, and so forth.

7. Calculate the required rooms department income. The sum of pretax profits, fixed charges and management fees, undistributed operating expenses, and other operate department losses less other operated department income equals the required rooms department income. The Hubbart Formula, in essence, places the overall financial burden of the hotel of the rooms department.

8. Determine the rooms department revenue. The required rooms department income, plus rooms department direct expenses of payroll and related expenses, plus other direct operating expenses, equals the required rooms department revenue.

9. Calculate the average room rate by dividing rooms department revenue by the expected number of rooms to be sold.

Forecasting Room Availability

The most important short-term planning performed by front office managers is forecasting the number of rooms available for sale on any future date. Room availability forecasts are used to help manage the reservations process and to guide front office staff in effective rooms management. Forecasting may be especially important on nights when a full house (10% occupancy) is possible.

A room availability forecast can also be used as occupancy forecast. Since there is a fixed number of a room in the hotel, forecasting the number of rooms available for sale and the number of rooms expected to be occupied forecasts the occupancy percentage expected on a given date. Room occupancy forecasts can be useful to the front office manager attempting to schedule the necessary number of employees for an expected volume of business. These forecasts may be helpful to other hotel department managers as well. For example, the housekeeping department needs to know how many rooms are expected to be occupied to properly schedule room attendants. Restaurant managers need to know the same information to better schedule service staff. The chef needs this figure to determine how much food to order for the restaurant.

Forecasting is a difficult skill to develop. The skill is acquired through experience, effective record keeping, and accurate counting methods. Several types of information can be. helpful in room availability forecasting:

- ❖ A thorough knowledge of the hotel and its surrounding area
- ❖ Market profiles of the constituencies the hotel services
- ❖ Occupancy data for the past several months and for the same period of the previous year
- ❖ Reservation trends, and a history of reservation lead times (how far in advance reservations are made)
- ❖ A listing of special events scheduled in the surrounding geographical area
- ❖ Business profiles of specific groups booked for the forecast dates
- ❖ The number of non-guaranteed and guaranteed reservation and an estimate of the
- ❖ The percentage of rooms already reserved and the cut-off date for rooms blocks
- ❖ The impact of citywide or multi-hotel groups and their potential influence on the
- ❖ Plans for remodeling or renovating the hotel that would change the number of
- ❖ Construction or renovating plans for competitive hotels in the area.

The process of forecasting room availability generally relies on historical occupancy data. To facilitate forecasting, the following daily occupancy data should be collected:

- ✓ Number of expected room arrivals
- ✓ Number of expected room walk-ins
- ✓ Number of expected room stayovers (rooms occupied on previous nights that will continue to be occupied for the night in question)
- ✓ Number of expected room no-shows
- ✓ Number of expected room under stays (check-outs occurring before expected departure date)
- ✓ Number of expected room check-outs
- ✓ Numbers of expected room overstays (checkouts occurring after the expected departure date)

These data are important to room availability forecasting since they are used in calculating various daily-operating ratios that help determine the number of available rooms for sale. Ratios are a mathematical expression of a relationship between two numbers that results from dividing one by the other. Most statistical ratios that apply to front office operations are expressed as percentages. The ratios examined in the following sections are percentages of no-shows, walk-ins, understays, and overstays.

Percentage of No-shows: $\dfrac{\text{Number of room No-shows}}{\text{Number of room Reservations}}$

Percentage of Walk-ins: $\dfrac{\text{Number of room walk-ins}}{\text{Total Number of room Arrivals}}$

Percentage of Overstays: $\dfrac{\text{Number of overstay Rooms}}{\text{Forecast Formula or Room Availability}}$

Once relevant occupancy statistics have been gathered, the number of rooms available for sale on any given date can be determined by the following formula:

$$\frac{\text{Number of Room Stayovers}}{\text{Number of Room reservations}}$$

$$\frac{\text{Number of Room Reservation x Percentage}}{\begin{array}{c}\text{Number of Room Understays}\\\text{Number of Room Overstays}\end{array}}$$

Sample Forecast Forms

The front office may prepare several different forecasts depending on its needs. Occupancy forecasts are typically developed on a monthly basis and reviewed by food, beverage, and rooms division management to forecast revenues, project expenses, and develop labor schedule.

Ten Days Forecast

The ten-day forecast at most lodging properties is developed jointly by the front office manager and the reservations manager, possibly in conjunction with a forecast committee. A ten-day forecast usually consists of:

- ❖ Daily forecasted occupancy figures, including room arrivals, room departures, room sold, and number of guests

- ❖ The number of group commitments, with a listing of each group's Name, arrival and departure dates, number of rooms reserved, number of guests, and perhaps quoted room rates

- ❖ A comparison of the previous period's forecasted and actual room counts and occupancy percentage.

A special ten-day forecast may also be prepared for food and beverage, banquet, and catering operation. This forecast usually includes the expected number of guests, which is often referred to as the house count.

To help various hotel departments plan their staffing and payroll levels for the upcoming periods, the ten-day forecast should be completed and distributed to all department offices by mid-week for the coining period. This forecast can, be especially helpful to the housekeeping department.

A three-day forecast is an updated report that reflects a more current estimate of room availability. The three day forecast is intended to guide management in fine tuning labor schedules and adjusting room availability information.

Room Count Consideration :

Control books, charts, Computer applications, projections, rauos and formulas can be essential in short and long range rooms count planning. Each day, the front office performs several physical counts of room occupied, vacant, reserved, and due to check out to complete the occupancy statistics for that day.

It is important for front desk agents to know exactly how many rooms are available, especially if the hotel expects to operate near 100% occupancy.

Budgeting For Operations

The most important long-term planning function performed by front office managers is budgeting front office operations. The hotel's annual operations budget is a profit plan that addresses all revenue sources and expense items. Annual budgets are commonly divided into monthly plan, which, is turn, are divided into weekly plans. These budget pans become standards against which management can evaluate the actual results to operation.

The budget planning process requires the closely coordinated efforts of all management personnel. White the front office manager is responsible for room's revenue forecasts, the hotel accounting division will be counter on to supply department managers with statistical information essential to the budget preparation process. The hotel general manager and controller typically review departmental budge plans and prepare a budget report for approval by the hotel's owners. If the budget is not satisfactory, elements requiring change may be returned to the appropriate division managers for review and revision. The primary responsibilities of the front office manager in budget planning are forecasting rooms revenue and estimating related expenses. Rooms revenue is forecasted with input from the reservations manager wile expenses are estimated with input from all department managers in the rooms division.

Forecasting Room Revenue

Historical financial information often serves as the foundation on which front office managers build rooms revenue forecasts. One method of rooms revenue forecasting involves an analysis of rooms revenue from past periods.

Another approach to forecasting rooms revenue bases the revenue projection on past room sales and average daily room rates.

Most expenses for front office operations are direct expenses in that they vary in direct proportion to rooms revenue. Historical data can be used to calculate an approximate percentage of rooms revenue that each expense item may represent. These percentage figures can then be applied to the total amount of forecasted rooms revenue, resulting in dollar estimates for each expense category for the budget year.

Typical rooms division expenses are payroll and related expenses; guestroom laundry (terry and linen); guest supplies (bath amenities, toilet tissue, matches); hotel merchandising (in room guest directory and hotel brochures); travel agent commissions and reservation expenses; and other expenses. When these costs are totaled and divided by the number of occupied rooms, the cost per occupied room is determined.

Since most front office expenses vary proportionately with rooms revenue, another method of estimating these expenses is to estimate variable costs per room sold and then multiply these costs the number of rooms expected to be sold.

Redefining Budget Plans

Departmental budget plans are commonly supported by detailed information gathered in the budget preparation process and recorded on worksheets and summary files. These documents should be saved to provide an explanation of the reasoning behind the decision made while preparing departmental budget plans. Such records may help resolve issues that arise during the budget review.

If no historical data are available for budget planning, other sources of information can be used to develop a budget. For example corporate headquarter can often supply comparable budget information to its chain affiliated properties. Also, national accounting and consulting firms usually provide supplemental data for the budget development process.

Many hotels refine expected results of operations and revise operations budgets as they progress through the budget year. Re-forecasting is normally suggested when actual operating results start to vary significantly from the Operations budget. Such variance may indicate that conditions have changed since the budget was first prepared and that the budget should be brought into line.

Evaluating Front Office Operations

Evaluating the results of front office operations is ah important management function.

Without thoroughly evaluating the results of operations, managers will not know whether the front office is attaining planned goals. Successfully front office managers evaluate the results of department activities on a daily, monthly, quarterly, and yearly basis. Important tools that front office managers can use to evaluate the success of front office operations.

- ✓ Daily operations report
- ✓ Occupancy ratios
- ✓ Rooms division income statement

The daily operation report, also known as the manager's report, the daily report, and the daily revenue report, contains a summary of the hotel's financial activities during a 24-hours period. The daily operations reports provide a means of reconciling cash, bank accounts, revenue, and accounts receivable. Daily operations reports are uniquely structured to meet the needs of individual hotel properties.

Rooms statistics and occupancy ratios form an entire section of a typical daily operation report. The information provided by the daily operations report is not restricted to the front office manager or hotel general manager. Copies of the daily operations report are generally distributed to all department and division managers in the hotel.

Occupancy Ratios

Occupancy ratios measure the success of the front office in selling the hotel's primary product: guestroom. The following rooms statistics must be gathered to calculate basic occupancy ratios:

- ❖ Number of rooms available for sale
- ❖ Number of rooms sold
- ❖ Number of guests
- ❖ Number of guest per room
- ❖ Net rooms revenue

Generally, these data are contained on the daily operations report. Occupancy ratios that can be computed from these data include occupancy percentage, average daily rate, multiple (or double) occupancy ratio, and average rate per guest.

The night auditor typically collects occupied rooms data and calculates occupancy ratios, while the front office manager analyzes the information to identify trends, patterns, or problems.

Occupancy Percentage

The most commonly used operating ratio in the front office is occupancy percentage. Occupancy percentage indicates the proportion of rooms either sold or occupied to number of rooms available during a specific period of time. Including complimentary rooms in the calculation can change certain operating statistics, such as average room rate. Using rooms sold, rooms occupied, or both are valid, depending upon the needs and history of the property. For purpose of this discussion, rooms occupied will be used to illustrate the occupancy percentage calculation.

Sometimes out-of-order rooms may be included in the number of rooms available. At properties that evaluate management performance partly on the basis of occupancy percentage, including out-of-order rooms in the number of rooms available provides the manager with incentive to get those rooms fixed and recycled more quickly. Including all rooms in the property also provides a consistent base on which to measure occupancy.

Conversely, not including out-of-order rooms may allow managers to artificially increase the calculated occupancy percentage simply by improperly classifying unsold rooms as out-of-order. Some properties do not include out-of-order rooms because the rooms are not actually available for sale. To the extent that the occupancy percentage is used to evaluate the performance of front office staff having no control over out-of-order rooms, including those rooms may unfairly penalize staff. Regardless of the approach chosen, it should be used consistently.

Most front office managers calculate an average daily rate (ADR) even through room rates within a property vary significantly from single rooms to suites, from individual guests to groups and conventions, from weekdays to weekends, and from busy to slack seasons.

$$\text{Average daily rate} = \frac{\text{Room revenue}}{\text{Number of Rooms Sold}}$$

Some hotels include complimentary rooms in the denominator to show the true effect of complimentary rooms on the average daily rate. Sometimes this is called the average house

Average Rate Per Guest

Resort hotels, in particular, are often interested in knowing the average room rate per guest (ARG). This rate is normally based on every guest in the hotel, including children.

$$\text{Average Rate per Guest} = \frac{\text{Rooms Revenue}}{\text{Number of Guests}}$$

Yield Management

The Concept of Yield Management

The concept of yield management originated in the airline industry. Most travellers know that passengers on the same flight often pay different fares. What is not as widely known is the potential application of yield management to other service industries. Yield management has proven successfully in the lodging, car rental, cruise line, railroad, and touring industries- basically, in situations where reservations are taken for a perishable commodity. The key to successful implementation appears to be an ability to monitor reservations and to develop reliable forecasts.

Yield management is based on supply and demand. Price tends to rise when demand exceeds supply; conversely, prices tend to fall when supply exceeds demand. Proper pricing adjustments, which take existing demand into account and can even influence it, appear to be the key to profitability. The hotel industry's focus is shifting from high-volume bookings to high-profit bookings. By increasing bookings on low-demand days and by selling rooms at higher room rates on high-demand days, the industry improves its profitability. In general, room rates should be higher (in order to maximize rate) when demand exceeds supply and lower (in order to increase occupancy) when supply exceeds demand.

Hotel Industry Applications

All hotel companies have a common problem: they produce a fixed Inventory of perishable products that cannot be stored if unsold by a specific time. The commodity that hotels sell is time in a given space. If a room goes unsold on a given night, there is not way to recover the time lost and therefore the revenue lost. Therefore these products are typically sold for varying prices that depend on the timing of the transaction and the proposed date of delivery. In the hotel industry, yield management is composed of a set of demand- forecasting techniques used to determine whether room rates should be lowered and whether a reservation request should be accepted or rejected in order to maximize revenue. Front office managers have successfully applied such demand lorecasting strategies to room reservation systems, management information systems, room and package pricing, looms and revenue management, seasonal rate determination, pre theater dinner specials, and special, group, tour operator, and travel agent rates. Front office managers have identified several benefits, including:

- ❖ Improved forecasting
- ❖ Improved seasonal pricing and inventory decision
- ❖ Identification of new market segments
- ❖ Identification of market segment demands
- ❖ Enhanced coordination between the front office and sales divisions

- ❖ Determination of discounting activity
- ❖ Improved development of business plans.
- ❖ Establishment of a value based rate structure
- ❖ Initiation of consistent customer- contact scripting (i.e. planned responses to customer inquires or requests regarding reservations)

Yield management seeks to maximize revenue by controlling forecast information in three ways: capacity management, discount allocation, and duration control.

Capacity Management

Capacity management involves various methods of controlling and limitation room supplies, balances the risk of overselling guestrooms against the potential loss of revenue arising from room spoilage (rooms going unoccupied after the hotel stopped taking reservations for a given date). Other forms of capacity management include determining how many walk-ins to accept on the day of arrival, given project

Discount Allocation

Discounting involves restricting the period and product mix (rooms) available at reduced or discounted rates. For each discounted room type, reservations are requested at various available rates, each set below rack rate. The theory is that the sale of a perishable item (the guestroom) at a reduced room rate is often better than no sale at all. The primary objective of discount allocation is to protect enough remaining rooms at a higher rate to satisfy the projected demand for rooms at that rate, while at the same time filling rooms that would otherwise have reminded unsold.

A second objective of limiting discounts by room type is to encourage upselling. In an upselling situation a reservation agent, or front desk agent, attempts to place a guest in a higher rated room. This technique requires a reliable estimate of price elasticity and/or the probability of upgrading. (Elasticity refers to the relationship between price and demand).

Duration Control

Duration control places time constraints on accepting reservations in order to protect sufficient space for multi-day requests. This means that, under yield management, a reservation for a one-night stay may be rejected, even though space is available for that night. These strategies may be combined. For example, duration control may be combined with discount allocation. A three-night stay may be available for discount, while a one-night stay may require the rack rate. It must be cautioned, though, that using these strategies must not be apparent to the guest. It would be difficult to explain to guest why he or she must stay three nights to get a discounted rate if he or she wants to stay only one night. Proper use of yield management relies on selling; it never divulges the yield management strategy being used.

Measuring Yield

Yield management is designed to measure revenue achievement. The yield statistic is the ratio of actual revenue to potential revenue. Actual revenue is the revenue generated by the number of rooms sold. Potential revenue is the amount of money that would be received if all room were sold at their rack rate.

of course, most hotel pricing systems arc not that simple; rack rates typically differ by occupancy and room type. Some properties calculate their potential revenue as the amount that would be earned if all rooms were sold at the double occupancy rate. Other properties calculate their potential revenue by taking into account the percentage mix of rooms normally sold at both single and double occupancy. The second method results in a lower total potential revenue figure, since single rooms are assumed to be sold at less than double rooms. While it is unlikely that a hotel will attain a potential that is based on 100% double occupancy (first method), a hotel using the second method may actually be able to exceed its "potential" if demand for double rooms exceeds sales mix projections.

Since the hotel's yield statistic will vary with the method used, once a preferred method has been chosen, it should be used consistently.

The mathematical computations required for yield management are relatively simple, even though a series of formulas are usually involved.

Formula 1: Potential Average single Rate

Potential average single rate - Room Revenues at Rack Rate.

Formula 2: Potential Average Double Rate

Potential avera e double rate - Double Room Revenues at Rack Rate Number of Rooms Sold as Doubles.

Formula 3: Multiple Occupancy Percentage

Rate Spread = Potential Average Double Rate - Potential Average Single Rate .

Formula 4: Rate Spread

Formula 5: Potential Average Rate

Potential Average Rate = (Multiple Occupancy Percentage x Rate Spread) + Potential Average Single Rate.

Formula 6: Room Rate Achievement Factor

$$\text{Achievement Factor} = \frac{\text{Actual Average Rate}}{\text{Potential Average Rate}}$$

Formula 7: Yield Statistic

$$\text{Yield} = \frac{\text{Actual Rooms Revenue}}{\text{Potential Average Rate}}$$

Yield= Room Nights Sold ^ Actual Average Room Rate Room Night's Available Potential Average Rate.

3 Yield= Occupancy Percentage x Achievement Factor Yield = Occupancy Percentage x Achievement Factor.

Formula 8: Identical Yields

Identical Yield Occupancy Percentage = Current Occupancy Percentage x - ^urrent ^ate Proposed Rate.

Formula 9: Equivalent Occupancy

Rack Rate - Marginal Cost.

Equivalent Occupancy = Current Occupancy Percentage x .

Rack Rate x (1-Dis. Percentage)-Marginal.

Formula 10: Required Non-Room Revenue Per Guest

Required Non-Room Revenue = $\dfrac{\text{Required Increase in Net Non-Room Revenue}}{\text{Number of Additional Guests / CMR}}$

All elements of yield management should be viewed together in order to make an appropriate decision. While the process is potentially complex, a failure to include relevant factors may render yield management efforts less than fully successful.

Yield statistics should be tracked daily. Tracking yield statistics for an extensive period of time can be helpful to trend recognition. However, to use yield management properly, management must track yield statistics for future days. Future period calculations must be done every business day, depending on how far in advance the hotel books its business. Discounts may be opened to raise occupancy or closed to raise average rates. If achieving full potential room revenue is not possible (and it usually is not), the front office manager must decide on the best combination of rate and occupancy.

Each sales contract for group business should be reviewed individually. Contracts should be compared with historical trends as well as with budgets. A hotel usually has a group sales target or budgeted figure for each month. If current transient demand is strong and the group will produce only minimal revenue, the hotel may consider not booking it. If demand is weak, the hotel may decide to accept the group simply to create revenue by selling rooms that would not otherwise be sold. Using group booking pace analyses will help management determine whether the hotel is on track to reach its target.

Another factor is the actual group-booking pattern already on the books. For example, a hotel may have two days between groups that are not busy. Management may solicit a lower-revenue-generating group to fill the gap. The opposite may also occur. A group may desire space during a period when the hotel is close to filling its group rooms goal. Adding the group may move the hotel group sales above its goal. While this appears to be favorable, it may displace higher-rated transient business.

The same type of analysis is needed for transient business. For example, due to the discounts offered by the hotel, corporate and government business may be assigned the standard category of rooms. As these standard rooms fill, the hotel may only have deluxe rooms left to sell. If demand is not strong, management may decide to sell the deluxe rooms at the standard rack rate to remain competitive. It is best to look at a combination of group and transient business before making firm occupancy and rate decisions.

Since the objective of yield management is to maximize revenue, tracking business by revenue source helps determine when to allow discounted room rates.

Potential High And Low Demand Tactics

A hotel needs to determine yield management strategies for both high and low demand periods. During times of high demand, the normal technique is to increase room revenue by maximizing average room rate. Transient and group business market segments may each require a unique, specific strategy.

Below are some transient business tactics used during high demand periods.

Try to determine the right mix of market segments in order to sell out at the highest possible room rates. This strategy is highly dependent upon accurate sales mix forecasting.

Monitor new business bookings and use these changed conditions to reassign room inventory. As occupancy begins to climb, consider closing out low room rates. Management should be prepared to re-open lower room rates should demand begin to slack off. Management must closely monitor demand and be flexible in adjusting room rates.

Consider establishing a minimum number of nights per stay. For example, a resort that always fills over Labor Day weekend may require a three- day minimum stay in order to

A number of group business tactics may be appropriate during high demand periods. When deciding between two or more competing groups, for example, select the group the produces the highest total revenue. Management must rely on its experience with groups to develop sound yield management policies.

Another tactic for handling group business during high demand periods is to attempt to move price-sensitive groups to low demand days. In other words, if the hotel forecasts high demand for a time when a price sensitive group has already booked space, management may try to reschedule the group's business to a period of lower demand.

The underlying strategy for transient and group business during low demand periods is to increase revenue by maximizing occupancy. Front office managers may find the following business tactics helpful.

- ❖ Carefully design a flexible rating system that permits sales agents to offer lower rates in certain situations. Such rates should be determined early in the planning process in anticipation of low demand periods.

- ❖ Strive to accurately project expected market mix. The precision of this projection will influence the eventual yield statistic.

- ❖ Management should closely monitor group bookings and trends in transient business. Do not close off lower rate categories and market segments arbitrarily.

- ❖ As low occupancy periods become inevitable, open lower rate categories, solicit price-sensitive groups, and promote corporate, government, and other special discounts. Consider developing new room rate packages and soliciting business from the local community (for example, weekend gateways for the local transient market)

- ❖ Consider maintaining high room rates for walk-in guests. Since these guests have not contacted the hotel prior to arrival, they typically present an opportunity to increase the average rate through top-down upselling techniques.
- ❖ A non-financial tactic involves upgrading guests to nicer accommodations than they are entitled to by virtue of their room rate, technique may lead to increased guest satisfaction and enhanced customer loyalty. The implementation of this policy is strictly a management decision.

Yield Management Computer Software

Although the individual tasks of yield management can be performed manually, the most efficient means of handling data and generating yield statistics is through a computer.

Yield management software does not make decisions for managers. It merely provides information and support for managerial decisions. Computer can store, retrieve, and manipulate large amounts of data on a broad range of factors influencing room revenue. Over time, yield management software can help management create models that produce probable results of decisions. Decision models are based on historical data, forecasts, and Those industries where computer-based yield management has been applied, the following results have been observed:

- ❖ **Continuous Monitoring:** a computerized yield management system can track and analyze business conditions 24 hours a day, seven days a week.

4* **Consistency:** software can be programmed to respond to specific changes in the market place with specific corporate or local management rules resident in the software.

- ❖ **Information Availability:** yield management software can provide improved management information, which, in turn, may help managers make better decisions more quickly.
- ❖ **Performance Tracking:** a computer-based system is capable of analyzing sales and revenue transactions occurring within a business period to determine how well yield management goals are being achieved.

Yield management software is also able to generate an assortment of special reports. The following are representative of yield management software output:

4* **Market Segment Report:** provides information regarding customer mix. This information is important to effective forecasting by market segment.

- **Calendar / booking graph:** presents room-nights demands and volume of
- **Future Arrival Date Status Report:** furnishes demand data for each day of the week. This report contains a variety of forecasting information that enables the discovery of . occupancy trends by comparative analysis of weekdays. It can be designed to

4* **Single Arrival Date History Report:** indicates the hotel's booking patterns (trends in reservations). This report relates to the booking graph by documenting how a specific day was constructed on the graph.

Weekly Recap Report: contains the sell rates for rooms and the number of rooms authorized and sold in marketing programs with special and/or discounted rates.

4- Room Statistics Tracking Sheet: tracks no-shows, guaranteed no-shows, walk-ins, and turn away. This information can be instrumental in accurate forecasting.

In-House Sales

Maximizing potential sales in all profit centers of the hotel is important as the hotel industry grows more sophisticated with emphasis for delivering quality services. Additional sales to in-house guests in the form of future reservations, in-house dining, room service etc. will assist in producing more profit for the hotel. The front office plays a key role in promoting these sales, and the FOM must develop and implement as plan to optimize the sales opportunities available to the front office staff.

The Role of The Front Office in Marketing And Sales

The front office is often seen as an information source and a request center for guests and hotel employees. For eg. producing the room sales forecast, blocking rooms for groups, greeting the guests and other operational activities.

However, today more than ever, hotel management demands more of the front office. The change in the nature of the front office role from a passive order-taker to an active order- generator or sales department, challenges the FOM to review the front office staffs established routine. They need to figure out the best way to direct the energies of the staff to support the efforts of the marketing & sales dept. At the beginning most FOMs would say this is a difficult task to achieve. Established routine are comfortable and less stressful. However, the FOM is a member of the management team and will need to interact with front office staff as a plan is developed.

Planning a Point-of-Sale Front Office

To plan a point-of-sale front office, the front office staff must promote the other profit centers of the hotel. This planning includes setting objectives, brainstorming ares for promotion, evaluating alternatives, drawing up budgets and developing an evaluation tool for feedback. Without a plan, a point-of-sale front office will have little chance of being successful. This plan should be developed in consultation with hotel management, departmental managers, and front-line employees from various departments. Team members are selected to assist in ensuring that a workable, profitable plan is developed.

To adopt a sales dept attitude, the following are some goals:

i. Sell rooms to walk-ins

ii. Upsell or Sellup to reservation holders

iii. Know your product

iv. Convey information to guests about other products

v. Ensure that maximum revenue is generated from sale of rooms by striking a balance between overbooking and a full house.

vi. Obtain guest feedback.

The front office staff can convey valuable information about the guest, essential for formulating effective marketing strategy. Changing market conditions require that such information be used by the marketing & sales dept.

Set Objectives

As a FOM who wants to develop a plan for a point-of-sale front office must set realistic objectives. The ultimate goal of sales-oriented front office is to increase the revenue from room sales, food and beverage sales and sales in other hotel departments. Developing objectives is carried out in consultation with the GM and other departmental managers.

Brainstorm Areas for Promotion

When developing a program to increase front office sales activity, the FOM in conjunction with other departmental managers and employees, should identify as specifically as possible the products and services to be promoted. An outline of promotional areas would be as follows:

1. **Front Office**
   i. Reservations- Upselling when reservation is placed, Additional reservations
   ii. Rooms- Upgrading during registration, promotional package
   iii. Secretarial services- Photocopies, dictation, typing, fax
   iv. Personal services- babysitting, shopping, concierge, bell staff
   v. Restaurants- Spl menu, Signature menu items, Spl pricing combinations table
   vi. Room Service- Meals, Early bird BF service, party service, snacks, alcohol
   vii. Lounge- Specials of the day, promotional package, featured entertainer
   viii. Clothing, toiletries
   ix. Souvenirs
   x. Promotional sales

2. **Health Facilities**
   i. Swimming pool-Availability to guests, membership
   ii. Jogging paths and group runs
   iii. Health Club-Availability to guests, membership

Evaluate Alternatives

Planning teams have to determine which concepts produced in a brainstorming session warrant further consideration. This is not always an easy task but if the team refers to stated goals and objectives, then the job is much easier. In this case, the overall purpose of the program would be to maximize sales by the front office staff, F&B dept, gift shop and health facilities products and services. The team must make the decision on which areas would be most profitable.

Incentive Programs

The point-of-sale plan should include an incentive program, which entails understanding employees motivational concerns and developing opportunities for employees to achieve their goals. This will encourage cooperation among the front-line employees who will implement the POS plan.

The FOM is responsible for determining how each employee is motivated. Many motivational strategies require a financial commitment by management. Motivation, understanding employee needs and desires and developing a framework for meeting them, is an essential part of developing a POS front office. Once the FOM knows what the employees want, he or she must develop a means of meeting these needs in return for the desired behaviour. The FOM must work with the GM and HRM to develop effective programs that meet their employee needs.

The objectives of the sales incentive program for front office employees is to encourage them to promote products and services in various areas of the hotel, including F&B dept, gift shop and the health facilities. Eg. Upgrading a reservation during registration, selling a meal in the hotel's restaurant, selling a room service product

Training Programs For A POS Front Office

Training is required to allow the successful delivery of sales techniques. The objective of training is to develop and teach employees methods to use to promote various profit centers of the hotel. Confidence in selling will develop if the POS program is introduced gradually giving the employee a chance to try out various techniques. Incentive programs

often overlooked but very effective practice is to allow front office employees to experience the services and products they sell. Training concepts for each of the areas listed on the promotion target outline must be detailed. Employees should receive suggestions on to say and when to say it timing is an important part of the sales opportunity.

playing episodes on video-tape of the front desk agents promoting products and within the hotel to the guest is an extremely effective training procedure. The only need to highlight simple approaches to presenting opportunities that enhances the guest experience.

Budgeting For a POS Front Office

The FOM will incur costs in operating a POS front office, including expenses involved in implementing incentive programs, producing training materials and spending time to plan. These costs, while not meant to be too high should be anticipated. If all appropriate steps are the income from increased sales should far exceed the additional costs. This projection related expenses is very useful when deciding which marketing ideas to explore.

Feedback

Feedback on the evaluation of the success of the front office in promoting other areas of the hotel is an important consideration in preparing a POS front office program. FOMs will not be able to know exactly how effective this promotional strategy is, but they must make every effort to obtain as much feedback from the staff and guests as possible. This information will be very valuable in planning future promotional ideas, incentive programs and training programs.

The standard guest test is one in which an outsider acts as a plant is hired by the hotel to experience hotel services and report the findings to the management. This test will enable the FOM to evaluate the sales performance of the front office staff.

When the management prepares the written information on tht guest comment cards, questions concerning alternative promotion targets should be listed. Choices offered by the hotel staff may be included in the report. This information provides feedback as to whether the suggestions were made and how they were received.

Another method of evaluating the program is check the actual financial results i.e. to determine whether the anticipated profits outlined in the budget is achieved. Use of VIP Guest Card indicates to the revenue earning outlet supervisor that the front office staff referred the guest Similar types of controls will enable the management to pinpoint the origins of room reservation, gift shop purchases and other sales. A record keeping system must be established to reflect the amount of money awarded to front office employees as incentives to increase sales in targeted areas.

Front Desk Statistics

Statistics are facts expressed in terms of rupees, numbers, figures, etc. and is the grouping of data in an orderly and usable manner. Ratios are generally expressed in terms of percentage.

1. % of Occupancy or Room Occupancy %

$$\frac{\text{No. of rooms sold}}{\text{No of rooms available for sale}} \times 100$$

2. Double Occupancy %

$$\frac{\text{House Count - No. of rooms sold}}{\text{No. of rooms sold}} \times 100$$

2 x No. of rooms sold - House Count No. of rooms sold

3. House Count

HC = Previous HC + Arrivals - Departures OR

Total guests = Single rooms + 2 x Double rooms + extra beds

4. Bed Occupancy %

$$\frac{\text{No. of beds sold}}{\text{No. of beds available for sale}} \times 100$$

5. Average Room Rate (ARR)

$$\frac{\text{Total Room Revenue}}{\text{No. of Rooms sold}}$$

6. Average Revenue per Guest / Average Spend

Total Room Revenue No.ofguestsstaying int hehotel(HC)

7. Overstay %

$$\frac{\text{No. of verstays,}}{\text{Total No. of scheduled departures}} \times 100$$

8. Understay %

$$\frac{\text{Understays}}{\text{Stayovers}} \times 100$$

9. No-show %

$$\frac{\text{No. of No-shows}}{\text{No. of Reservations}} \times 100$$

10. Cancellation %

$$\frac{\text{No. of cancellations}}{\text{No. of Reservations}} \times 100$$

11. Foreign Guests %

No. of Foreign guests in the hotel ^

Total guests in the hotel (HC)

12. Overbooking Percentage Rate (OPR)

No. of rooms overbooked x 100 Total Rooms available for sale

13. Walk-In %

$$\frac{\text{No. of Walk-ins}}{\text{Rooms committed}} \times 100$$

14. Yield %

$$\frac{\text{Actual Revenue}}{\text{Potential Revenue}} \times 100$$

15. Room Count

Total Available rooms - Total vacant rooms

OR

PNO + Reservations - Departure rooms

16. RevPAR = Total Available Rooms

Glossary

A

ACCESSIBLE PARKING SPACE: A parking space, specially designed for disabled persons, that meets or exceeds the requirements of the people with Disabilities Act. It should have a minimum width of 13 feet (4 meters)-8 feet (2.4 meters) for the vehicle and 5 feet (1.5 meters) for an access aisle.

ACCESSIBLE ROUTE: A route that connects the accessible parking area to an accessible entrance of the building the parking lot serves. An accessible route should be a minimum of 36 Inches (91 centimeters) wide and have no abrupt surface transitions (from sidewalks to streets, for example) or obstructions that would present hazards to a visually Impaired person.

ADJOINING ROOMS: Guestrooms located side by side without a connecting door between

ADR Index: ADR of selected hotel/ADR of that hotel's competitive set **AFFILIATE RESERVATION SYSTEM:** A hotel chain's reservation system in which all participating properties are contractually related. Each property is represented In the computer system database and Is required to provide room availability data to the reservation center on a

AFFILIATED HOTEL: A hotel that Is a member of a chain, franchise, or referral system. Membership provides special advantages, particularly a national reservation system. **AIRLINE-RELATED GUESTS:** Airplane crew members and passengers who need

AIRPORT HOTEL: A hotel located near a public airport. Although airport hotels vary widely In size and service levels, they are generally full-service and are more likely than other hotels to have In-room movies, computerized property management systems, and call accounting systems.

ALL-EXPENSE TOUR: A tour offering all or most services—transportation, lodging, meals, sight-seeing, and so on for a pre-established price. The terms "all-expense" and "all-inclusive" are much misused. Virtually no tour rate covers everything. The terms and conditions of a tour contract should specify exactly what is covered.

ALL-SUITE HOTEL: A hotel that features suites. A suite Is an accommodation larger than the typical hotel room, with a living space separate from the bedroom. A suite can also have a kitchenette or whirlpool.

ALTERNATIVE TOURISM: Smaller scale tourism in terms of the number of tourists and the dimensions of tourism development. Sometimes called responsible or green tourism. **AMBIANCE:** (1) A feeling about or an Identity for an establishment created by the combination of decor, lighting, furnishings, and other factors.

(2) Applied to environments, a feeling or mood associated with a particular place, person, or thing; an atmosphere.

AMENITY: Service or item offered to guests or placed in guestrooms for the comfort and convenience of guests, and at no extra cost. Examples are various guest services (such as In-room entertainment systems, automatic check-out, free parking, concierge services, and multilingual staff) in addition to an array of personal bathroom Items offered by most hotels and motels. Amenities are designed to Increase a hotel's appeal, enhance a guest's stay, and encourage guests to return.

AMERICAN HOTEL & MOTEL ASSOCIATION (AH&MA): A federation of state and regional hotel associations that offers benefits and services to hospitality properties and suppliers. AH&MA reviews proposed legislation affecting hotels, sponsors seminars and group study programs, conducts research, and publishes Lodging magazine. The Educational Institute of AH&MA is the world's largest developer of hospitality industry training materials, including textbooks, videotapes, seminars, courses, and software.

AMERICAN PLAN: A room rate that Includes three meals.

ATRIUM: A guestroom floor configuration In which rooms are laid out off a single-loaded corridor encircling a multistory lobby space; also the multistory lobby space, usually with a

ATTRITION: Difference between original room request and the actual purchase of a group.

AUTOMATED WARE-UP: system in which guests or F.O. staff may use the hotel's telephone system to program a prerecorded call to be received In a guest's room at a time

AUTODIAL/AUTO-ANSWER/AUTO ATTENDENT: In electronic communications, a feature of sophisticated modems that enables a user to place a call to a pre-specified phone number at an exact time, or set up the modem In a ready state to receive incoming calls.

AUTOMATIC FORM NUMBER READER (AFNR): A feature of a guest check printer that facilitates order entry procedures; Instead of a server manually Inputting a guest check's serial number to access the account, a bar code Imprinted on the guest check presents the check's serial number in a machine-readable format.

AUTOMATIC IDENTIFICATION OF OUTWARD DIALING: A feature of a call accounting system that immediately identifies the extension from which an outgoing call is placed.

AUTOMATIC ROOM/RATE ASSIGNMENT: Computerized assignment made through algorithms based on parameters specified by hotel management officials. Rooms may be selected according to predetermined floor zones (similar to the way In which guests are seated in a dining room), or according to an index of room usage and depreciation.

AUTOMATIC ROUTE SELECTION: A feature of a call accounting system that provides the capability of connecting with a variety of common carriers.

AUTOMATIC SLIP FEED (ASF): A feature of a guest check printer that prevents overprinting of items and amounts on guest checks.

AUTOMATIC SPELL CHECK: A computer program that helps users proofread documents by automatically checking for spelling errors. The words In the document are electronically compared with entries in the spell checker's dictionary. When a word which appears in the document does not appear In the program's dictionary, it is generally highlighted on the display screen so the operator can correct it.

AVAILABILITY FORECAST: Estimate of a number of rooms that remain to be sold.

AVERAGE OCCUPANCY: A ratio that shows rooms sold over a fixed period of time as a percentage of total available rooms In a property over the same period of time.

AVERAGE OCCUPANCY PER ROOM: A ratio that shows the average number of paid guests for each room sold. Calculated by dividing number of paid room guests by number of rooms sold. Measures management's ability to use the lodging facilities.

AVERAGE ROOM RATE/AVERAGE DAILY RATE(ARR/ADR): A ratio that indicates average room rate, and to what extent rooms are being up-sold or discounted; calculated by dividing rooms revenue by number of rooms sold. Also called average daily rate or ADR.

B

BACK OF THE HOUSE: The functional areas of a hotel or restaurant In which employees have little or no direct guest contact, such as kitchen areas, engineering and maintenance,

BED & BREAKFAST (B&B): A small Inn or lodge that provides a room and a breakfast. Often a B&B Is In a residential home setting and/or a historic building converted to a quaint

BENCHMARKING: Search for the best practices and an understanding of how they are achieved In efforts to determine how well a hospitality organization is doing.

BILLED-TO- ROOM CALL: An operator-assisted call that allows guests to have an operator place their calls and then advise the hotel of the charges.

BLACKOUT DATE: Any day in which the hotel will not honor a negotiated rate.

BLOCK/GROUP BLOCK: Rooms reserved exclusively for members of a specific group.

BOOKING ENGINE: An online system used by hotels that allows prospective hotel guests to check availability and make reservations at the hotel.

BUSINESS MIX: A hotel's desired blend of business from various segments such as business transient, corporate group, leisure, and convention.

BRAND LOYALTY: Interest of guests or potential guests to revisit and recommend a hotel or restaurant.

BUCKET CHECK: Systematic examination of guest folio to ensure the accuracy of information like rate verification, credit monitoring, and confirmation of departure date.

C

CABANA: A guestroom adjacent to the pool area, with or without sleeping facilities.

CALL ACCOUNTING SYSTEM: A system that is part of the telephone equipment that prices telephone calls made by hotel guests and sends the Information to the property management system (PMS) for billing.

CALL-AROUND: Telephone "shopping" technic in which a hotel staff calls competitive hotels to enquire about room rates and availability.

CAMP/PARK LODGE: Sleeping acco. In parks and other nature conservation areas owned by govt, agencies

CANCELLATION: A reservation voided by a guest.

CANCELLATION HOUR: A specific time after which a property may release for sale all unclaimed non-guaranteed reservations, according to property policy.

CANCELLATION NUMBER: A number Issued to a guest who properly cancels a reservation, proving that a cancellation was received and acted upon.

CARD KEY: A plastic card, resembling a credit card used In place of a metal key to open a guestroom door. Card keys require electronic locks.

CASINO HOTEL: A hotel that features legal gambling, with the hotel operation subordinate to the gambling operation.

CENTER CITY HOTEL: Full-service hotel located In a downtown area.

CENTRAL RESERVATION OFFICE: Part of an affiliate reservation network. A central reservation office typically deals directly with the public, advertises a central (usually toll-free) telephone number, provides participating properties with necessary communications equipment, and bills properties for handling their reservations. CENTRAL RESERVATION SYSTEM: CRS- An external reservation network. See also Affiliate Reservation System and Non-Affiliate Reservation System.

CENTRALIZED ACCOUNTING SYSTEM: Financial management system that collects accounting data from one or more hotels and combines and analyzes the data at different site.

CHAIN OPERATING COMPANY: A firm that operates several properties, such as Holiday Inn Worldwide or Hilton Hotels Corporation. Such an operator provides both a trademark and a reservation system as an Integral part of the management of its managed properties.

CHARTER: To hire the exclusive use of any aircraft, vessel, or other vehicle.

CHARGE BACK: Credit card charges reversed when a cardholder successfully protests the legitimacy of the charge

CHECK-IN: The procedures for a guest's arrival and registration.

CHECK-OUT: (1) The procedures for a guest's departure and the settling of his or her account. (2) A room status term Indicating that the guest has settled his or her account, returned the room keys and left the property.

CITY LEDGER: Set of accounts used to record charges to and payments from a hotel's non-registered guests

COMMERCIAL AGENCY: A travel agency that specializes in commercial business and usually has little or no walk-in clientele.

COMMERCIAL FOOD SERVICE OPERATION: An operation that sells food and beverages for profit. Independent, chain, and franchise properties are all commercial food service operations.

COMMERCIAL HOTEL: A property, usually located In a downtown or business district, that caters primarily to business clients. Also called a transient hotel.

COMMERCIAL TRAVEL: Travel for business purposes, not for pleasure.

COMPLIMENTARY OCCUPANCY PERCENTAGE: A ratio that shows the percentage of occupied rooms that are complimentary and generate no revenue; calculated by dividing complimentary rooms for a period by total available rooms for the same period. Sometimes referred to simply as complimentary occupancy.

COMPLIMENTARY ROOM/COMP: A complimentary or "comp" room is an occupied room for which the guest is not charged. A hotel may offer comp rooms to a group In ratio to the total number of rooms the group occupies. One comp room may be offered for each fifty rooms occupied, for example.

CONCIERGE: An employee whose basic task is to serve as the guest's liaison with hotel and non-hotel attractions, facilities, services, and activities.

CONDOMINIUM HOTEL/CONDO/CONDOTEL: A hotel In which an Investor takes title to a specific hotel room, which remains In the pool to be rented to transient guests.

whenever the investor Is not using the room. The Investor expects to receive a gain from the increase In value of the hotel over time, as well as receive ongoing Income from the

CONDUCTED TOUR: (1) A pre-arranged travel program, usually for a group, that Includes escort service. (2) A sight-seeing program, such as a city tour, conducted by a

CONFERENCE CENTER: A specialized hotel, usually accessible to major market areas but in less busy locations, that almost exclusively books conferences, executive meetings, and training seminars. A conference center may provide extensive leisure facilities.

CONFIRMED RESERVATION: An oral or written statement by the supplier (a carrier, hotel, car rental company, etc.) that he or she has received and will honor a reservation. Oral confirmations have virtually no legal worth. Even written or telegraphed confirmations have specified or Implied limitations. For example, a hotel is not obligated to honor a confirmed reservation if the guest arrives after 6 p.m., unless late arrival is specified. Confirmed reservations may be either guaranteed or non-guaranteed.

CONNECTING ROOMS: Two or more guestrooms with private connecting doors permitting guests access between rooms without their having to go Into the corridor.

CONSORTIA RATE: Room rate given to a guest whose room is booked by selected travel agencies

CONTINUOUS QUALITY IMPROVEMENT (CQI): Ongoing efforts within the hotel to better meet the guests' expectations and to find ways to work with better, less costly and faster methods.

CONTINENTAL BREAKFAST: A small morning meal that usually includes a beverage, rolls, butter, and jam or marmalade.

CONTINENTAL PLAN: A room rate that includes continental breakfast.

CONVENTION HOTEL: Lodging property with extensive and flexible meeting and exhibition spaces.

CORPORATE HOTEL CHAIN: Hotel organization that has Its own brand or brands, which may be managed by the corporate chain or by a conglomerate.

CREDIT MANAGER: Person responsible for establishing and enforcing the hotel's credit policies.

CROSS TRAIN: Tactic of training persons for more than one position so that they can assist whenever they are needed.

CRUISE SHIPS: Passenger ships designed for vacationers. Today's cruise ships feature a variety of activities and entertainment and can be thought of as floating resort hotels.

CRUISE-ONLY AGENCY: A travel agency that sells only cruises.

CUTOFF DATE: Date on which unreserved rooms held In a group block are returned to the

D

DAY RATE: A special room rate for less than an overnight stay.

DIRECT FLIGHT: A journey on which the passenger does not have to change planes.

DISPLACEMENT: To substitute one source of revenue for another.

DOMESTIC TOURISM: Travel within the traveler's country of residence.

DOUBLE: (1) A guestroom assigned to two people. (2) In beverage operations, a drink prepared with twice the standard measure of alcohol In one glass.

DOS/DOSM: Director of sales/ Director of Sales and Marketing

DOUBLE OCCUPANCY RATE: A rate used for tour groups that bases the per-person charge on two to a room.

DOUBLE-LOADED SLAB: A guestroom floor configuration in which rooms are laid out on both sides of a central corridor.

DOUBLE-LOCKED ROOM: An occupied room for which the guest has refused housekeeping service by locking the room from the Inside with a dead bolt. Double- locked rooms cannot be accessed by a room attendant using a standard passkey.

DUMP RATE: Hotel term for significantly reducing room rates for a given date or dates.

E

EARLY ARRIVAL: A guest who arrives at the property before the date of his or her reservation.

EARLY MAKEUP: A room status term Indicating that the guest has reserved an early check-in time or has requested his or her room to be cleaned as soon as possible. ECO-TOURISM : Low-Impact tourism that avoids harming the natural or normal environment. In this relatively new approach to promoting enjoyment, as well as protection, of the environment, tourists seek out environmentally-sensitive travel and/or tours or vacations which, In some way, Improve or add to their knowledge of an environment.

ESCORT: A person, usually employed by a tour operator, who accompanies a tour from departure to return and serves as guide, trouble-shooter, etc.

ESCORTED TOUR: A group of travellers traveling with a guide who has travel experience and has set up an Itinerary for the group.

EMERGENCY REPORT/DOWN TIME REPORT: Information and lists that would be critical in the event of a disaster or a PMS crash.

EMPOWERMENT: Act of granting authority to employees to make key decisions within the employees' area of responsibility.

EUROPEAN PLAN: A room rate that does not include any meals.

EXECUTIVE FLOOR: A floor of a hotel that offers exceptional service to business and other travellers. Also called a business floor or the tower concept.

EXPECTED ARRIVAL/DEPARTURE REPORT: A daily report showing the number and names of guests expected to arrive with reservations, as well as the number and names of

EXPECTED ARRIVALS LIST: A daily report showing the number of guests and the names of guests expected to arrive with reservations.

EXPECTED DEPARTURES LIST: A daily report showing the number of guests expected to depart, the number of stay-overs (the difference between arrivals and departures), and the names of guests associated with each transaction.

EXPRESS CHECKOUT: Guest initiated checkout that do not require guests to be physically present at the hotel's front desk for folio payment.

EXTENDED STAY HOTEL: Mid-price, limited-service hotel, marketing to guests desiring accommodations for extended time periods.

F

FADE (RATE)/FLEX RATE: Reduced rate authorized for use when a guest seeking a reservation exhibits price(rate) resistance.

FAMILIARIZATION (FAM) TOUR: A reduced-rate, often complimentary, trip or tour offered to travel agents, wholesalers, incentive travel planners, travel writers, broadcasters, or photographers to promote fa hotel or a destination.

FAMILY LIFE CYCLE: A series of stages used to distinguish between types of travellers; variables used to determine family life cycle stages are age, marital status, and presence and ages of children.

FAMILY RATE: A special room rate for parents and children occupying one guestroom.

FLASH REPORT: Daily Information provided to the GM that reports key financial information from the previous day and often accumulated data for the month and/or YTD compared with the actual data from previous years.

FOLIO: Detailed list of guestroom and other charges authorized by the guest or legally imposed by the hotel.

FOREIGN INDEPENDENT TOUR (PIT): A tour created for Individuals or families who walk Into a travel agency and tell an agent what country or area they would like to visit and what they would like to see and do there.

FRONT DESK: The focal point of activity within the hotel, usually prominently located In the hotel lobby. Guests are registered, assigned rooms, and checked out at the front desk.

FRONT DESK AGENT: A hotel employee whose responsibilities center on the registration process, but also typically include preregistration activities, room status coordination, and mail, message, and Information requests.

FRONT OF THE HOUSE: The functional areas of a hotel or restaurant In which employees have extensive guest contact, such as the front desk (In hotels) and the dining room(s).

FRONT OFFICE: A hotel's command post for processing reservations, registering guests, settling guest accounts, and checking guests In and out.

FRANCHISE: Arrangement whereby one party (the brand) allows another party (the hotel owners) to use Its logo, name, systems and resources in exchange for a fee.

FULL- SERVICE AGENCY: A travel agency that handles all types of travel for consumers.

FULL-SERVICE HOTEL: A hotel with a full range of services and amenities which may include some or all; onsite restaurant and lounge, meeting facility, pool, fitness center, business center, etc. Compare Economy/Limited-Service Hotel.

GLOBAL DISTRIBUTION SYSTEM (GDS): A network of Internet reservation systems that provide a central place where travellers and travel agents can check availability and reserve travel related products like hotels, airline, car rentals, cruises, rail. Formed and managed by the airline Industry and includes system like Same, Apollo, Amadeus, Pegasus. GOPPar : (Gross Operating Profit per available room): Avg. ross profit (revenue less management controllable expenses) generated by each gues room during a given time period. GRAND TOUR, THE: An extended trip across the European continent that served as part of the education of young British aristocrats. A typical tour began In England and had the major cultural cities of Italy as Its destination. In Its early years, a tour could last as long as 40 months. By the end of the Grand Tour era, the age of the traveler had increased, and the length of the tour decreased; Individuals traveled more for pleasure than for an extended educational tour. The Grand Tour era lasted from about 1500 to 1820.

G

GROUP PICK-UP: The guestrooms that are actually rented by a group that are help In a Group Reservation.

GROUP RESERVATIONS: A block of multiple guestrooms that are being held under an individual or business name at a particular hotel for a specific date or range of dates. Generally used for conventions, conferences, meetings, receptions, weddings, etc.

GUEST COMMENT CARD: Short questionnaires that lodging properties and food service establishments ask their guests to fill out. Guest comments are used by the property to define current markets and to Improve the operation.

GUEST HISTORY CARD: A record of the guest's visits including rooms assigned, rates, special needs, and credit rating.

GUEST HISTORY FILE: A file containing guest history cards. It Is maintained for marketing purposes and Is referred to for return visits.

GUEST INFORMATION SERVICES: Automated information devices ip public hotel areas that enable guests to obtain Information about in-house events and local activities.

GUEST LEDGER: A type of ledger that consists of Individual records (called folios) of the hotel's registered guests, The guest ledger provides current status on guest charges and payments; the front office Is responsible for summarizing these transactions during the guest's stay. A guest ledger may also be referred to as a front office ledger; transient ledger, or room ledger.

GUEST MIX: The variety and percentage distribution of hotel guests - individual, group, business, leisure, and so on—who stay at a hotel or patronize a restaurant.

GUEST PROFILE: A list of the characteristics that a property's guests have in common. The guest profile helps management to Identify which market segments the property appeals to and which segments the property wants to attract.

GUEST RELATIONS: The establishment of personal rapport and goodwill with guests through service and attention to individual guest needs. In a narrower sense, the promotion of In-house products and services, the entertainment of VIPs, and the handling of social functions—especially In a resort hotel.

GUARANTEED RESERVATIONS: A reservation that Is guaranteed by the guest to be paid even If the guest falls to arrive. Often this guarantee Is made by a company or with a credit card.

GUEST SERVICE MANAGER (GSM): Manager of the guest services department.

GUEST SERVICE REPRESENTATIVE (GSR): Employees who provide check-in checkout, mall, key, message, and Information services for guests.

GUEST SURVEY: A questionnaire completed by guests and used by managers to define current markets and to improve the operation. Managers may talk with guests through the survey or leave the questionnaires with them to fill out. Questionnaires may be long, and some questions may require detailed answers.

GUESTROOM CONTROL BOOK: A book used to monitor the number of guestrooms committed to groups. It controls guestroom booking activity by providing the sales office with the maximum number of guestrooms it can sell to groups on a given day. The remaining guestrooms (and any unsold guestrooms allotted to groups) are available for individual guests.

GUESTROOM KEY: A key that opens a single guestroom door if it is not double-locked.

GUESTROOM'MAINTENANCE: A form of preventive maintenance Involving the inspection of a number of Items in the guestroom; minor lubrication of doors and other equipment, repair of obvious small problems and, when needed, the Initiation of a work order for more substantial problems or needs.

H

HIA (HIGH-SPEED INTERNET): Technology required to allow hotel guests to access the Internet at download speeds much higher than those that can be achieved with traditional telephone dial-up systems.

HOSPITALITY: The cordial and generous reception of guests. Derived from the Latin term hospes, "a guest."

HOSPITALITY INDUSTRY: Lodging and food service businesses that provide shortterm or transitional lodging and/or food.

HOSPITALITY SUITE: A room used for entertaining (e.g., a cocktail party); usually a function room or parlor.

HOTEL: A large lodging facility, generally a hotel Is full service and a multi-story building with interior entrance guest rooms.

HOTEL CHAIN: A group of affiliated hotels.

HOTEL GUEST CYCLE: The sequence of phases that begins with pre-sale events, continues through point-of-sale activities, and concludes with post-sale transactions. The phases Identify the physical contacts and financial exchanges that occur between guests and various revenue centers within a lodging operation.

HOTEL MANAGEMENT COMPANY: A company that Is hired to professionally manage

HOTEL REPRESENTATIVE: An individual who offers hotel reservations to wholesalers, travel agents, and the public. A hotel representative or "rep" may be paid by the hotels he or she represents on a fee basis or by commission. Many hotel reps also offer marketing and other services.

HOT SPOT: Wi-Fi area that allows for high-speed Internet access or other data transmission.

HOUSE LIMIT: A guest credit limit predetermined by management officials.

HOUSE ACCOUNT: Account whose entries are assessed to another hotel entity such as sales and marketing dept, GM or the FOM

HOUSE COUNT: Total number of guests staying In a hotel on a specific night.

HVAC SYSTEM: Heating, Ventilating and Air-conditioning system

I

INCENTIVE TRAVEL: Travel financed by a business as an employee incentive.

INCIDENTAL CHARGES: Guest charges on a folio or bill for items other than room and tax such as; food, beverage, phone, movies, etc.

INCLUSIVE TOUR: A tour in which specific elements—air fare, hotels, transfers, etc. — are included for a fiat rate. An Inclusive tour rate does not necessarily cover all costs.

INDEPENDENT FOOD SERVICE OPERATION: An operation owned by an owner or owners with one or more properties having no chain relationship. Menus, food purchase specifications, operating procedures, etc. may differ among the owned properties.

INDEPENDENT HOTEL: A hotel with no chain or franchise affiliation. It may be owned by an individual proprietor or a group of Investors.

IN-ROOM CHECK-OUT/IN-ROOM VIDEO CHECKOUT: A computer-based check-out procedure that provides guests with a way to access and review their folio data and approve and settle their accounts In their rooms. The technology Involves Interfacing the guestroom telephone, the television, and an in-room computer with the property management system's guest accounting module.

IN-ROOM GUEST CONSOLE: A multi-feature phone that may include such functions as two-way speakerphone capability; a jack for portable computer use; an alarm clock; radio; remote control of heating, ventilating, and air conditioning, television, and room lights; energy management; and a theft alarm.

IN-ROOM MOVIE SYSTEM: Guestroom entertainment provided through a dedicated television pay channel. Charges for the use of this In-room entertainment are posted to the

INTRANET: Designated segment of an organization's Internet site where access and use is restricted to specifically Identified Individuals, (employees or managers)

K

KING BED: A bed approximately 78 inches by 80 inches.

KIOSK: Small electronic unit (machine) located in the lobby that allows guests with proper Identification to register or checkout of the hotel without the need to Interact with.

L

LANAI: A guestroom with a balcony or patio, overlooking water or a garden. LANDMARK: Distinguishing feature that stands out and provides a reference point for orientation. Landmarks also provide travellers with Information about direction and distance.

LATE ARRIVAL: A guest holding a reservation who plans to arrive after the property's designated cancellation hour and so notifies the property.

LATE CHARGE: Charged purchase made by a guest that is posted to the guest's folio after the guest has settled his or her account.

LATE CHECK-OUT: A guest who is being allowed to check out later than the property's standard check-out time.

LIMITED SERVICE HOTEL: A lodging facility that offers no or very few amenities, services or extra facilities such as restaurants, pools, meeting rooms, etc. Generally an inn or motel is limited service.

LONG-TERM STAY/RELOCATION GUESTS: Those individuals or families relocating to an area who require lodging until permanent housing can be found.

LODGE: A lodging facility that Is generally small and often designed in located In a rustic outdoors environment or activities such as; fishing, skiing, boating, eco-tours.

LODGING FACILITY: A business that rents guestrooms to the public on a nightly or shorter term range of dates, i.e. weekly, month to month.

LODGING INDUSTRY: Lodging and food service businesses that provide short-term or transitional lodging.

LUXURY HOTEL: A hotel with high room rates that features exceptional service and amenities.

M

MASS TOURISM: Wide-scale travel by a large number of people — not just the elite- brought about by the Increase In leisure time, discretionary Income, and reliable and inexpensive modes of transportation such as the automobile and airplane.

MASS TOURISTS: Travellers participating In wide-scale travel designed for large numbers

MASTER FOLIO: A bill that all charges for the members of a group are posted to.

MASTER KEY: A key that can open all guestroom doors that are not double-locked.

MARKET SEGMENTATION: Efforts to focus on highly defined smaller group of travellers

MID-PRICE/EXTENDED-STAY HOTELS: Hotels that caters mostly to persons who must be In an area for a week or longer. The guestrooms of mid-price/extended-stay hotels have more living space than regular hotel guestrooms, and may also have cooking facilities. Guestrooms In these hotels tend to be less expensive than guestrooms in fu.ll-

MID-RANGE SERVICE: A modest but sufficient level of service that appeals to the largest segment of the traveling public. A mid-range property may offer uniformed service, airport limousine service, and food and beverage room service; a specialty restaurant, coffee shop, and lounge; and special rates for certain guests.

MINI-BAR: A small, under-the-table unit that can be stocked with liquor, beer, and wine, usually located within a hotel room for the convenience of guests.

MISSION STATEMENT: More focused picture of what the hospitality operation wants to do and how It will do it.

MLO: MINIMUM LENGTH OF STAY-Designation that instructs the reservationists to decline a reservation request from any guest who will not reserve a room for the minimum number of days allowed as predetermined by the hotel.

MODIFIED AMERICAN PLAN: A room rate that includes one or two meals usually breakfast and dinner.

MOT-MOMENT OF TRUTH: Any and every time a guest has an opportunity to form an Impression about the hospitality organization. MOT can be positive or negative and may, but do not have to, involve the property's staff members.

MOTEL: A smaller lodging facility, generally a motel is limited service and one to two stories with exterior entrance rooms that guest can drive up to. Often referred to as motor hotel.

MULTIPLE GUEST SPLITS: Charges that are to be divided among a group of guests.

MULTITASKING: Productivity Improvement tactic in which an employee does more than one thing at a time.

MYSTERY SHOPPER SERVICES: Method of product and service evaluation In which a person poses as a guest, experiences the products and services provided, and reports on the perceived quality of products and services received during the visit.

N

NEGOTIATED RATE AGREEMENT: Document that details the specific contractual obligations of a hotel and client when the hotel has offered and the client has agreed to a negotiated rate.

NET ADR YIELD RATE: ADR actually received by a hotel after subtracting the cost of fees and assessments associated with a room sale. The formula Is:

Net ADR Yield= Room Rate - Reservation Fees/ Room Rate Paid

NIGHT AUDIT: Process of reviewing for accuracy and completeness the accounting transactions from one day to conclude, or close, that day's sales Information in preparation for posting

NO-SHOW: Guest who makes a room reservation but fails to cancel the reservation or arrive at the hotel on the date of an /al.

O

OCCUPANCY REPORT: A report prepared each night by a front desk agent that lists rooms occupied that night and also lists those guests expected to check out the following day.

OCCUPANCY INDEX: A ratio measure computed as - Occupancy Rate of a selected hotel/Occupancy rate of that hotel's competitive set

OFF-THE -SHELF: Term relating to a generic product (eg training resource) that Is developed for general use rather than for a unique property

ON-CALL: Agreement between a hotel employer and a staff member, who will remain available to work during a specified time period

ON-THE -BOOKS: Hotel term for cumulative current data.

ONLINE RESERVATION SYSTEM: An Internet based system used by hotels that allows prospective hotel guests to check availability and make reservations at the hotel.

OUT-OF-ORDER: A room status term Indicating that a room cannot be assigned to a guest. A room may be out-of-order for maintenance, refurbishing, deep cleaning, or other reasons.

OVERBOOKING: Accepting reservations that exceed available rooms.

OVERSTAY: A guest who remains at the property after his or her stated departure date.

OVERFLOW(hotel): Guestrooms that are a part of a larger group booking that cannot be accommodated by a single hotel.

P

PACKAGE: A special offering of products and services created by a hotel to increase sales. There are weekend packages, honeymoon packages, sports packages, and so on.

A typical package might, for a special price, include the guestroom, meals, and the use of the property's recreational facilities.

PACKAGE TOUR: A tour put together by a tour packager or operator. Travellers who buy the package make the trips by themselves rather than with a large group. The package offers, at an inclusive price, several travel elements which a traveler would otherwise purchase separately — any combination of lodging; sight-seeing; attractions; meals; entertainment; car rental; and transportation by air, motor coach, rail, or even private vehicle. A package tour may Include more than one destination, paid

OCCUPANCY PERCENTAGE: A ratio that Indicates management's success In selling Its product; calculated by dividing number of rooms sold by the number of available rooms.

POINT OF SALE SYSTEM (POS): A computerized system that retail outlets such as restaurants, gift shops, etc, enter orders and maintains various accounting Information. The POS generally interfaces with the property management system (PMS).

PROPERTY MANAGEMENT SYSTEM (PMS): A computerized front desk system that manages hotel room inventory, guest billing end Interfaces with various other systems such as telephone, call accounting, point of safe (POS), entertainment, etc.

PROPRIETARY BOOKING ENGINE: A Internet reservation system that Is owned and operated by an individual hotel or group of hotels to allow them to take reservation on their own website without paying a fee to the GDS, th rd party booking engines or franchise reservation systems.

PICKUP: Actual no. of guestrooms reserved for individuals. Group pickup is the no. of guestrooms reserved In a group block.

PULL-OUT: Industry term for an In-room sofa that converts to a bed.

Q

QUAD: A guestroom assigned to four people; may have two or more beds.

QUALITY GROUP: The group of travellers for whom the quality of their vacation Is of paramount Importance. They want and are willing to pay for first-class accommodations and service.

QUEEN: A bed approximately 60 inches by 80 inches.

R

RACK RATE: The current rate charged for each accommodation as established by the property's management.

REGIONAL GETAWAY GUESTS: Guests who check into a hotel close to home In order to enjoy a weekend away from children or other responsibilities.

RESERVATIONS AGENT: An employee, either In the front office or in a separate department, who is responsible for all aspects of reservations processing.

RESERVATIONS DEPARTMENT: A department within a hotel's rooms division staffed by skilled telemarketing personnel who take reservations over the phone, answer questions about facilities, quote prices and available dates, and sell to callers who are shopping around.

RESIDENT MANAGER: The manager In charge of the rooms division in a mid-size to large hotel. Sometimes resident managers are also in charge of security.

RESORT HOTEL: A hotel, usually located in a desirable vacation spot, that offers fine dining, exceptional service, activities unavailable at most other properties, and many amenities.

RETAIL TRAVEL AGENT: An individual qualified to arrange and sell transportation and other travel services and products directly to the public.

RevPAR: A statistic used In the hotel industry used to measure revenue per available room. Total hotel room revenue divided by the total rooms available to rent for a day or range of dates.

RevPAR INDEX: Ratio measure computed as- Revpar of a selected hotel/ Revpar of that hotel's competitive set

ROOM BLOCK: An agreed-upon number of rooms set aside for members of a group

ROOM DATA CARD: A card used to record information concerning the basic characteristics and major elements of an individual guestroom.

ROOM INSPECTION: A detailed process in which guestrooms are systematically checked for cleanliness and maintenance needs.

ROOM NIGHT: One guestroom occupied for one night.

ROOM OCCUPANCY SENSOR: A device that uses infrared light or ultrasonic sound waves to sense the physical occupancy of a room. Sensors have the ability to turn on devices and appliances such as lights, air conditioning, and heating whenever a guest enters a space, and to turn these devices and appliances off when the guest leaves.

ROOM RACK: A card Index system that is constantly updated to reflect occupied and vacant rooms. In the evening, the room rack contains forms for only those registered guests remaining for the night who are to be charged for rooms. A daily room report can be prepared from the room rack.

ROOM RATE: The price a hotel charges for overnight accommodation.

ROOM STATUS: Information about current and future availability of guestrooms In a lodging property. Current availability Is determined through housekeeping data. Future availability Is determined through reservations data.

ROOM STATUS DISCREPANCY: A situation in which the housekeeping department's description of a room's status differs from the room status Information that guides the front desk employee In assigning rooms to guests. Discrepancies can seriously affect a property's ability to satisfy guests and maximize rooms revenue.

ROOMING LIST: A list of the guests who will occupy reserved accommodations. This list is submitted In advance by the buyer/travel agent.

ROOMS ACTIVITY FORECAST: Information on anticipated arrivals, departures, stay-overs, and vacancies. Managers use this forecast to determine staffing needs at the front desk and in housekeeping areas.

ROOMS ALLOTMENT REPORT: A report that summarizes rooms committed (booked or blocked), by future date.

ROOMS AVAILABILITY REPORT: A report that lists, by room type, the number of available rooms each day (net remaining rooms In each category).

ROOMS CHECKLIST: A list, used for guestroom (preventive) maintenance, of all the items In the guestroom with a brief notation opposite each Item of the type of Inspection, repair, lubrication, adjustments, or cleaning activity to be performed.

ROOMS DISCREPANCY REPORT: A report that notes any variances between front desk and housekeeping room status updates. It often alerts management to Investigate the possibility of sleepers.

ROOMS DIVISION: The largest, and usually most profitable, division In a hotel. It typically consists of four departments: front office, reservations, housekeeping, and

ROOMS HISTORY REPORT: A computer-based report that depicts the revenue history and use of each room by room type. This report Is especially useful to those properties employing an automatic room assignment function.

ROOMS MANAGEMENT MODULE: A front office application of a computer-based property management system. The module (a) maintains up-to-date information on the status of rooms, (b) assists In the assignment of rooms during registration, and (c) helps coordinate various guest services.

ROOMS PRODUCTIVITY REPORT: A report that ranks room types by percentage of occupancy and/or by percentage of total rooms revenue.

ROOMS STATUS REPORT: A report that indicates the current status of rooms according to housekeeping designations, such as: on-makeup, on-change, out-of-order, dean, and ready for Inspection.

ROI: Return on investment- percentage rate of return achieved on the money invested in a hotel property

ROLL-AWAY BED: A type of bed usually designed for use by a single guest, that can be easily transported from one room to another

ROOM-MIX: Ratio of the hotel's room types

ROOM NIGHT: Single night use of a guestroom

RYOKAN: Traditional Japanese lodging facilities featuring tatami mat floors and Japanese landscaped gardens.

S

SAINT JULIAN THE HOSPITALLER: The patron saint of innkeepers, travellers, and boaters.

SAINT NOTBURGA: The patron saint of food servers.

SHIFT MANAGER: The manager in charge of a casino during a period of time, usually a six- to eight-hour shift.

SHOULDER DATE: Hotel term for a day, or even a season, between two busier time periods.

SIDE-BY-SIDE SUITE: A suite that consists of two small bays, each with windows to the outside.

SINGLE BED: A bed approximately 36 Inches by 75 Inches.

SKIPPER: A guest who leaves without paying,

SLEEPER: A vacant room that Is believed to be occupied because the room rack slip or registration card was not removed from the rack when the previous guest departed.

SLEEP OUT: Industry term for a room Identified in PMS records as occupied, but that Is actually unoccupied.

SPA: A mineral spring, or a locality or resort hotel near such a spring, to which people resorted for cures (from Spa, a watering place In eastern Belgium). Today, the word spa is used more loosely to refer to any fashionable resort locality or hotel.

STAYOVER: A room status term Indicating that the guest Is not checking out and will remain at least one more night.

STUDIO: A guestroom having one or two couches that convert Into beds.

SUBURBAN HOTEL: A hotel that Is somewhat smaller than a downtown hotel (typically 250 to 500 rooms), Is usually part of a chain, and has restaurants, bars, and other amenities

SUITE: (1) A guestroom with a parlor area In addition to a sleeping room, and perhaps a kitchenette. (2) Several pieces of frimi are of similar design, usually sold together to outfit a

SUITE HOTEL: A hotel whose sleeping rooms have separate bedroom and living room or parlor areas, and perhaps kitchenettes.

SOP: Standard Operating Procedure/Practices- Policy or procedure that Is so routine It should be readily known and followed by all affected employees

T

TABLE D'HOTE: A full-course meal with limited choice at a fixed price.

THIRD PARTY BOOKING ENGINE: An Internet site that provides a booking engine where a traveler can search a large number of lodging facilities for availability and reserve a room. The lodging facilities are not amllated with the site and pays a fee for the business that the third party site generates. Examples of third party sites Include; hotels.com, priceline.com.

TOUR: Any pre-arranged (but not necessarily prepaid) journey to one or more places and back to the point of origin.

TOUR BROKER: An Individual licensed and bonded by the Interstate Commerce Commission to operate motorcoach tours In the United States and, In some cases, Canada, as permitted by the scope of his or her license. Also known as a motorcoach broker or tour operator.

TOUR OPERATOR: A business that puts together travel tours and sells them directly to individuals or through travel agencies.

TOURISM DEVELOPMENT: The long-term process of preparing for the arrival of tourists; entails planning, building, and managing attractions, transportation, accommodation; services, and facilities that serve the tourist.

TOURISM ENCLAVE: Self-contained resort complex that caters to all the needs of tourists who arrive as part of a tour or other type of package.

TOURISM PLANNING: The process of preparing for tourism development; a tool for addressing the choices associated with tourism development.

TOWER: A guestroom floor configuration In which rooms are grouped around a central vertical core.

TRANSIENT HOTEL: Lodging operation that caters primarily to business people; transient hotels tend to be busiest Monday through Thursday.

TRAVEL CLUB: A type of travel agency that charges an annual fee to Its members and in return offers packaged vacations to members at reduced prices.

TREMONT HOUSE: A 170-room Boston hotel that opened in 1829. It was the first hotel to have bellpersons, front desk agents, locks on guestroom doors, and free soap for guests. It Is considered the first modem American hotel.

TURNOVER RATE: Measure of proportion of a workforce that Is replaced during a designated time period. ETR=no. of employees separated/ No. of employees In the

TWIN: A guestroom with two twin beds.

TWIN BED: A bed approximately 39 inches by 75 inches.

U

UNDERSTAY: A guest who checks out before his or her stated departure date.

UPGRADE: To move to a better accommodation or class of service.

USALI: Uniform System of Accounts for the Lodging Industry- Standard set of accounting procedures used to record a hotel's financial transactions and and condition.

V

VILLAGE STAY: An alternative form of tourism in which the tourist can experience life In a rural place-fishing village, farm, historic village, etc. — by staying In the home of a resident, in a dormitory, or in some other type of accommodation.

VOICE MAIL: A system that is part of the telephone equipment which provides for hotel guests and staff to retrieve a messages left by a caller.

VIRTUAL TOUR: Streaming video located on a Web site that allows sections of a hotel in a 360° degree view.

W

WALK-IN GUEST: A guest who arrives at a hotel without a reservation.

WALKING A Guest: A situation In which a hotel Is unable to honor a guest's reservation and helps the guest find accommodation elsewhere.

WATERPARK HOTEL: A hotel that offers a large recreational water elements such large pools, multiple pools, slides or other water related venues.

WATS: Wide Area Telephone Service; a toll-free number pertaining to CRS

WARM- BODY SYNDROME: Often used but ineffective selection technique that Involves hiring almost anyone who applies for the vacant position, without regard to qualifications.

WI-FI: Wireless Fidelity- Internet access technology that does not use a a building's wiring system when providing users internet access.

WOW FACTOR: Feeling guests have as they experience an unanticipated extra during

X

X-REPORT: Term commonly used to Indicate the total revenue generated by a revenue

Y

YACHT CLUB: A private dub located near a large body of water, whose main purpose Is to provide facilities such as marinas to boat owners.

YIELD MANAGEMENT: A process or strategy that hotel operators use to maximize their hotel room revenue by achieving the right balance between room rates and occupancy that generates the most revenue.

YTD: Numbers that indude all revelant data for the current year

Z

Zero - Call (Oh CALL): A telephone canll placed with an operator's assistance. Examples may indude calling- and credit-card calls, collect calls and third-party calls.

Z REPORT: Term commonly used to Indicate the total revenue generated during an entire time period-typically a day.

Appendices

Front Office Forms

The front office relies on various forms or formats to monitor guest stay.

Pre-Arrivals

Since reservation starts the guest cycle, capturing and maintaining reservation data is critical to affective front office operation. Reservations are recorded on a reservation record on form or entered into a computer based reservation file.

The guest may be sent a letter of confirmation to verify that a reservation has been made and that its specifications are accurate. Confirmation permits errors in communication to be corrected before the guest arrival and verifies the guest correct mailing address for future correspondence.

Arrival

The front office may use a registration card or a computer based evaluation to check in guest. The registration card may contain blank spaces for the guest to fill in (as often found in non-automated or semi-automated properties) or may be pre-printed with the guest information from the computer file. Registration card requires the guest to furnish personal data and to indicate length of stay and method of settlement. Most hotels requite the guest signature on registration card before the relationship between the hotel and the guest is considered legal. Registration card may also be required by law to contain printed statement relating to the availability of safe storage for guest valuables.

Once the guest is registered the front office creates a guest folio or a statement of charges and credits incurred by the guest. In non-automated system a folio card contains a series of columns for recording debit entries, credit entries and current account balance. At the end of the business day each column of the folio is reviewed and the ending account balance is carried forward as the opening guest account balance for the following day.

In a semi-automated system, guest transactions are posted sequentially on a folio card. Data recorded includes the transaction date, the originating revenue center, the transaction amount and the resulting account balance.

In a fully automated system, electronic folios simplify transactions posting and handling. For a guest with a reservation personal data already stored in the computer are verified at registration or as part of pre-registration activity.

Walk-in guest account requires a front desk agent to enter the guest information during the registration process. Electronic folios are stored internally and can be printed on demand.

A voucher is a support document detailing the facts of transactions. Non-automated and semi-automated properties depend on vouchers to communicate information from remote revenue center to the front desk. A voucher is a support document and does not replace a source document created at the point of purchase.

Departure

Guest folio should be kept current throughout occupancy to ensure on accurate account balance for settlement at departure. In addition to the guest folio, other forms may be required for account settlement. A credit card voucher for example, will be needed if the guest wishes to pay by credit card.

	NIPS HOTEL KOLKATA	
	ROOM RESERVATION FORM	Sr. No.
Last Name :	Middle Name :	First Name :
Address :		
Arrival Date	Time	Arriving from	Arriving by
Departure Date :	Time :	Departing to :
Type of Accommodation : Single ☐ Double ☐ Twin ☐ Suite Exe. ☐ Floor ☐	Room Tariff
Mode of Payment Cash ☐   Credit Card ☐   TC ☐ Company ☐   Travel Agent ☐
Advance Deposit Rs.   Receipt No.   Dated :
Reservation Guaranteed : Yes ☐   No ☐ If Yes By : Cash ☐   Credit Card ☐   Others (Specify) ☐
Billing Instructions
Special Requests
Requested by : Telephone No.	Received by
Date	Confirmation No.

NIPS HOTEL
KOLKATA

AMENDMENT / MODIFICATION

Original Reservation

Reservation No.　　　Type of Rooms :　　　Pax :

Arrival Date :　　　　Departure Date :

Amended to

Type of Room :　　　Pax :　　　Room Tariff :

Arrival Date :　　　　　　　　Departure Date :

Reason for amendment :

Amendment Given by :　　　Telephone No.

Amendment Received by :　　　Date :

CALCELLATION

Cancelled by :

Address :

Telephone No.

Reason for Cancellation :

Date :　　　　　　　Time :

Received by :

NIPS HOTEL
KOLKATA

Sl. No. _____

Guest Registration Card

Name : _____
       (Surname)   (First name)

Designation : _____ Date of arrival in India : _____

Organization : _____ Duration of stay : _____

Address : _____ Arrival from : _____

Purpose of visit : Business Next destination : _____

Arrival date : _____ Conference   Leisure

Date of birth : _____ Departure Date _____

Arrival time : _____ Room No. _____

Passport details : _____ Nationality _____

Room rate : Rs. _____ Tax _____

Number of guest : _____ Room type _____

Passport number : _____

Date of issue : _____

Place of issue : _____

Mode of payment :

Cash _____ TA Voucher _____ Travelers Cheque _____

Credit card number _____

Expiry date : _____ Number _____ Date _____

Bill to company _____

Certificate of Registration No. _____ Issued at _____

(Only for foreign residents in India)

Signature Receptionist   *Guest Signature*

NIPS HOTEL
KOLKATA

Sl. No. _____
Date _____

Cash Receipt

Room No.	Particulas	Amount Rs.	P.
	Received with thanks from _____		
	Total		

Rupees : _____
_____

NIPS HOTEL
KOLKATA

Scanty Baggage

Date of Arrival	Room Number	Name of Guest	Name of Bellboy	Arrival Time	Description of Baggage	Remarks	Signature of Lobby Manager	Signature of Bellboy

---

NIPS HOTEL
KOLKATA

Safety Locker Form

Name : _____ Room Number _____

Permanent Address : _____

_____

Authorised Signature _____ Date _____

Keys delivered by _____

N.B. : A charge of Rs. 100/- will be made if the keys are lost.

www.ingramcontent.com/pod-product-compliance
Lightning Source LLC
LaVergne TN
LVHW070531070526
838199LV00075B/6753